Twelve on the River St. Johns

University of North Florida Press
Jacksonville

TWELVE

≈≈≈≈≈≈≈≈≈≈≈≈≈≈≈≈≈≈≈≈≈≈≈≈≈

on the
River St. Johns

Charles E. Bennett

The University of North Florida Press is a member of University Presses of Florida, the scholarly publishing agency of the State University System of Florida. Books are selected for publication by faculty editorial committees at each of Florida's nine public universities: Florida A&M University (Tallahassee), Florida Atlantic University (Boca Raton), Florida International University (Miami), Florida State University (Tallahassee), University of Central Florida (Orlando), University of Florida (Gainesville), University of North Florida (Jacksonville), University of South Florida (Tampa), University of West Florida (Pensacola).

Library of Congress Cataloging-in-Publication Data

Bennett, Charles E., 1910-
    Twelve on the River St. Johns.
    Bibliography: p.
    Includes index.
    1. Saint Johns River Region (Fla.)--Biography.
2. Florida--Biography. I. Title.
CT229.B46 1989 975.9'1 89-16428
ISBN 0-8130-0913-8 (alk. paper)
ISBN 0-8130-0948-0 (pbk.: alk. paper)

Orders for books published by all member presses should be addressed to University Presses of Florida, 15 NW 15th Street, Gainesville FL 32603.

Cover: The St. Johns River (1890-1900) by Martin Johnson Heade. Collection Cummer Gallery of Art, Jacksonville, Florida.

90-1284

Contents

Preface

I HAVE LIVED NEAR THE ST. JOHNS RIVER
during most of my lifetime, and I have grown to love its broad
expanses, its verdant banks, and its populated places. I have
also been intrigued with and inspired by the people who have
come to live near the river or on its banks. This book does not
include some of the most distinguished people who have lived
in the area because recent complete biographies about them
exist. Instances are René Laudonnière, Governor Napoleon
Bonaparte Broward, and Frederick Delius. I excluded others
who had no firm intention of permanent residence, such as
John James Audubon, Winslow Homer, and Stephen Crane.
All those included intended to be permanent residents of the
St. Johns area. All were achievers. Each had a unique quest.
Each drew strength from religious or benevolent insight.

I hope the readers of this book will find in its pages not only
pleasure but also inspiration from the lives of the strong people portrayed. I believe each story speaks of both the individual's spiritual life and the blossoming of American idealism.

Introduction

AMERICAN HISTORY IS A FOUR-HUNDRED-
year mosaic of the lives of its people. This book is a thin slice
of that history, from its beginnings in the sixteenth century
to today, told through the life stories of people who lived on
or near Florida's St. Johns River.

The St. Johns is Florida's greatest river and one of the
world's most beautiful. Spanish explorers who noted its exis-
tence early in the 1500s called it Río de Corrientes, River of
Currents. On 1 May 1562, French Protestants seeking a haven
rediscovered the river and called it the River of May to commemorate the date of their arrival and perhaps for its lush
subtropical beauty. When the Spanish recaptured the river in
1565, they renamed it for the saint whose feast day followed
the day of its capture, San Mateo. In the early seventeenth
century the river came to be called by the name of the mission
near its mouth, the San Juan. When the British acquired the
river in 1763, they kept that name, translated into English—
the St. Johns.

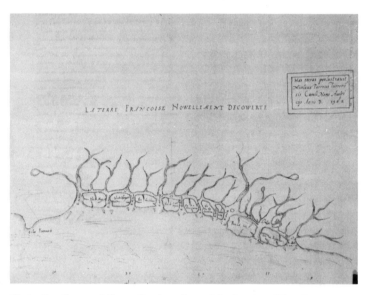

Nicolas Barré's map of the southeastern shore of the Americas ("New France"),
1562. Courtesy Museo Naval, Madrid.

ONE

~~~~~~

Saturiba

SATURIBA, KING OF THE TIMUCUAN INDI-
ans[1] in the mid-sixteenth century, ruled the area that includes
what is now Florida's St. Johns River valley. He headed an
alliance of thirty other chieftains that included ten of his
brothers (Bennett 1975, 76). His domain stretched along the
banks of the river the Indians called Welaka (Cabell and Hanna
1943, 4), identified on early Spanish maps as Río de corrietes
and later as Río de Corrientes (Cumming 1958, 113, 135), and
across the Florida and Georgia coastal plains. Saturiba had inherited his authority through his mother's royal bloodline, the
path the Timucuans believed to be the most reliable since the
ostensible father was not always the father in fact. The deci-
siveness, judgment, and charisma of the born leader combined
in Saturiba with physical strength and endurance and with
fierceness and cleverness in battle, making him the popular as
well as the legitimate choice as king. Frequent warfare on the
borders of his realm helped the Timucuan sustain his leadership and expand his kingdom.

1. Saturiba is the usual Spanish spelling, but he was also called by the Spanish Sotoriba or Saturiban; by the French, Satouriona, Saturiova, and Satrova;
by the English, Satoirioua. The Timucuan Indians occupied a large portion
of northeast and central Florida and some coastal and interior areas of Georgia
(Lowery 1959, 2:54, 59).

1

Timucuans prayed to the sun in a religion centered in nature and natural forces. "They have no knowledge of God or of any religion except that which appears to them, such as the sun and moon," a French observer would later report. "They have their priests in whom they have great faith because they are able magicians, diviners, and invokers of devils. These priests are their doctors and surgeons. The priests always carry with them a bag of herbs and drugs to administer to the sick who, for the most part, are syphilitic on account of their great love for the women and maidens whom they call daughters of the sun" (Bennett 1975, 13).

The Frenchman went on to describe Timucuan marriage practices. "Each man is married to one woman. The king is permitted to have two or three wives, but his first wife is the only one recognized as queen, and only her children inherit the property and authority of the father" (Bennett 1975, 13). Timucuan mores sometimes departed more radically from European practices. Saturiba's son, Athore, married his mother, an event that did not disturb the king's subjects because Saturiba had taken another wife and divorced himself from Athore's mother.

In Saturiba's middle years the religious turbulence coming to a head in France was to transform forever the Timucuans' familiar life of hunting, planting, and making love and war. The European Protestant movement born early in the century had reached the stage of armed civil rebellion. Catherine de Medici, the Catholic mother of France's King Charles IX, bowed to the urgings of her chief adviser, Admiral Gaspard de Coligny, to support the colonization of America by France's Protestants, the Huguenots. Sending the Huguenots to North America would not only provide them a refuge and put a damper on the civil strife in her own country but would also expand France's domain.

Thus twelve-year-old Charles IX sponsored the first recorded European landing at the Welaka (St. Johns) on 1 May 1562, although the eastern coast of Florida had been mapped as early as 1500 (Cumming 1958, 5) and Juan Ponce de León had landed about ten miles south of the river's mouth on 8 April 1513 (Lowery 1959, 1:139). (Spain had claimed all of North America and tried to establish settlements in Florida as early as 1521, but all her efforts north of Mexico had failed [Bennett 1968, xii–xiii].) The expedition's leader, Jean Ribault, commemorated the date of his arrival by naming the Welaka the River of May (Connor 1927, 70).

Saturiba watched from the river's south bank as Ribault offered a prayer and mingled with friendly Timucuans on the north bank.[2] When the French crossed the river, Saturiba moved from his main residence in an oak grove to meet them. To the landing boats beached on the south shore he sent his leading men with gifts of mulberries and blackberries. Then the king himself came forward, accompanied by some of his brothers and a crowd of warriors carrying bows and arrows. Their naked bodies bright with paint looked, according to Ribault, "right soldier-like" (Connor 1927, 71–72). The braves wore their long hair woven with grasses and trussed up like crowns. The French gave the Indians clothing, hatchets, cutting hooks, and other small tools, and to Saturiba and his brothers colorful robes.

The king then guided the French south and west from the riverbank into country Ribault described as "the fairest, frutefullest and plesantest of all the worlde, habonding in honey, veneson, wildfoule, forrestes, woodes of all sortes" (Connor 1927, 72).[3] On the heavily wooded high ground stood oak, palm, cedar, bay, pine, and centuries-old live oak trees, with startled birds and deer taking flight from every open space. To the west bright green marshlands stretched upriver to an eighty-foot bluff, a sight which, Ribault wrote, was "a pleasure not able to be expressed with tongue" (Connor 1927, 72). On their way back to the boats, Saturiba answered Ribault's probing questions with tales of gold, silver, copper, and precious gems to the northwest, in the Appalachian Mountains.

The next day the French erected on a hillock near the river a white marble column on which were carved the arms of

2. Today Mayport Naval Station stands on the south bank, and the north bank, where Ribault landed, is Fort George Island.

3. That the column was of white marble is noted in the report of Blas Merlo before the Alcalde of Bayamo, 1566, Archivo General de Indias, Justicia 212, translated by Eugene Lyon, in the files of the Fort Caroline National Memorial.

Mouth of the St. Johns, 1562. Engraving by Jacques Le Moyne De Morgues in his *Brevis Narratio* (Frankfurt: de Bry, 1591).

France, the letter "R," sign of the French monarch, and the date 1561, the year the expedition had been organized in France (Lowery 1959, 2:394; Connor 1927, 14, 110). Seated between two of his brothers, Saturiba watched from a nearby rise ceremonially strewn for the occasion with boughs of shining green magnolia leaves. All three men, well-built and athletic, wore their hair piled on their heads, decorated with fur which had been dyed red and fashioned into crowns. Attending the king, warriors in full battle dress sported freshly painted faces and feathers in their hair, their bows and arrows within easy reach. In light of the keen interest in metals shown by the French, Saturiba had ordered his men to deck themselves for this occasion with all the metal they possessed. One of his brothers wore hanging from his neck an ingeniously worked and highly polished plate of copper with a smaller silver disk at its center. Many of the warriors wore in one ear a small plate of copper, a device they used to scrape sweat and grime from their bodies. Saturiba assured Ribault that such metals could be found in abundance not more than five or six days away (Connor 1927, 80).

To celebrate and cement the Indians' new friendships, Saturiba ordered a feast set out for the French, who devoured the boiled crabs, shrimp, lobsters, and other fish roasted over open fires and served with hot cornmeal and baked beans. The guests declined the king's suggestion that they proceed to the Indians' homes some distance from shore to sample other delicacies. Instead, the French explained and demonstrated their guns, and in turn Saturiba gave Ribault and his second in command, René Laudonnière, several chamois skins painted in unusual designs and vivid colors (Bennett 1975, 18, 62). Some days later the French sailed away, delaying only briefly for an exploration upriver in small boats.

Two years later, on 25 June 1564, René Laudonnière returned from France with three hundred men, four of them with their wives and children, equipped to settle permanently on Timucuan land. Saturiba rushed to the shore to greet them crying out the word the French had taught him in 1562, "Ami! Ami!" He soon brought forward other Indians, all eager to welcome their old friends (Bennett 1975, 60). The king persuaded the French to accompany him to the river's mouth, where the marble column stood wreathed in magnolia garlands of dark polished leaves and waxy white blossoms. At its foot lay baskets of corn, pumpkins, fruit, edible and medicinal roots, and vessels of perfumed oils, all of which Saturiba pressed on Laudonnière. The Indians displayed their reverence for the column by kissing it and required the French to do likewise.

The French chose to build their fort or walled town, La Caroline (named for Charles IX), on the south bank of the River of May next to the high bluff Saturiba had pointed out to the first expedition. The king frequently visited the work, usually accompanied by his two sons and other Indians, all "offering to be of service," according to Laudonnière. The Frenchman gave Saturiba "various articles of merchandise so that he

René Laudonnière and Athore, son of Saturiba, in 1564 at the French marble column erected in 1562 at the mouth of the River of May. Watercolor on vellum by Jacques Le Moyne De Morgues is in the New York Public Library, bequest of James Hazen Hyde. Engraving (shown here) is from Le Moyne's *Brevis Narratio* (Frankfurt: de Bry, 1591).

would know the good will we bore to him and so that he would be anxious for our friendship. As the days went on our friendship and alliance increased in strength" (Bennett 1975, 72).

The Timucuan king showed particular interest in the moat being dug around the fort, and he took measurements of the walls "both inside and out." Then, "seeing that the earth was being taken from the ditch and formed into a rampart," he asked what purpose it served (Lorant 1946, 40). Advised that the earthworks were to protect the settlers, Saturiba said he would like to see the work completed, and he responded to Laudonnière's request for help by sending eighty of his strongest men to help complete the fort and the huts inside. One of the tasks Saturiba assigned them was to build roofs for the new French structures as they did for their own. "The Indians worked hard," Laudonnière reported, "some bringing palmetto leaves, and others weaving them together. In this way the order of their chief was carried out just as he wished it" (Bennett 1975, 72).

With his countrymen safe within the walled town, Laudonnière set out to investigate the possibilities that France's newest colony offered. He sent his lieutenant d'Ottigni to reconnoiter upriver into the territory of Saturiba's enemies, Olata Ouae Outina and the Thimogona Indians. Outina had forty subordinate ally or vassal Indian kings against Saturiba's thirty. From his principal village west of the River of May near the mouth of the Oklawaha, he regularly warred with Saturiba as well as with Potavou, Onetheaqua, and Houstaqua, who all lived near the path to the Appalachians. When Laudonnière assured Saturiba that he considered the Indian king's enemies his own, Saturiba provided two guides for the upriver reconnaissance. Laudonnière described the guides as "so anxious to fight with their enemies that they seemed as happy as if they were going to a wedding" (Bennett 1975, 73).

Although establishing a religious haven and expanding France's domain were perhaps the strongest motives behind settling the Fort Caroline colony, the discovery there of gold ore would be bound to ensure continuing support from France. Knowing this, Laudonnière required the colonists to hold for the French treasury all precious metals they obtained, and he put a good deal of energy into discovering where precious ores could be mined. He sent a second exploratory expedition to the Appalachians, from which the men returned with only a small amount of gold ore (Bennett 1975, 216n.12).

Nevertheless, the hope of securing the route to Appalachian gold led some of Laudonnière's lieutenants to promise Outina an alliance in his war against the Indians along that route. By the same reasoning, Laudonnière, too, saw little advantage in fighting Outina and put off Saturiba's request for help against his enemy by refusing to "purchase the friendship of one by the hatred of another" (Bennett 1975, 82): perhaps within two months, Laudonnière suggested, when foodstuffs had been collected and the barques were shipshape.

In response, Saturiba showed up at the fort with the fifteen hundred warriors he had gathered for his war on Outina. He could bring in only twenty men, he was told, a procedure easy for the French to enforce because the fort's single, narrow entrance was easily guarded. One of the colonists, artist Jacques Le Moyne, recorded that "Saturiba was disappointed, but he disguised his feelings well. He selected twenty of his followers, and with these he entered the fort, where he was shown everything. The sound of drums and trumpets and the reports of the brass cannon, which we fired in his presence, frightened him vastly. When he was told that all his men had run away, he could readily believe it, since he himself would gladly have been somewhere else. This incident, by the way, gave us a great reputation in the whole neighborhood; indeed, after this the natives believed us to be far more powerful than we actually were" (Lorant 1946, 42).[4]

Saturiba made preparations to go forward on his own, beginning with a ritual reported in detail by both Le Moyne and Laudonnière. "He asked the neighboring chiefs for assistance," Le Moyne wrote. "When they came, the whole force— in war paint and feathers—sat down in a circle, with Saturiba in their midst. A fire was lighted to his left, and two large vessels of water were placed at his right. The chief, rolling his eyes angrily and gesturing with his arms, raised a horrible yell. His men repeated the cry, striking their hips and rattling their weapons. Then Saturiba, taking a wooden bowl full of water, turned toward the sun, worshiped it, and prayed for victory over the enemy" (Lorant 1946, 57).

The king's preparations to this point had taken "at least a half hour," according to Laudonnière. Saturiba then "sprinkled water from his hands over the heads of the chiefs. . . . Furiously he threw the rest of the water on a fire which had been expressly made for that purpose. That done, he cried three times, 'He, Thimogona,' and was accompanied in this by more than five hundred Indians. They were all assembled there and cried out in unison, 'He, Thimogona.' According to one of the Indians this ceremony signified that Satouriona begged the sun to give him victory and happiness so that he could scatter

4. Besides his detailed account of his experiences in America, Le Moyne drew scores of fine pictures. An excellent two-volume work on his achievements is edited by Paul Hulton, *The Work of Jacques Le Moyne De Morgues* (London: British Museum Publications, Ltd., 1977).

the blood of his enemies as he had scattered the water at his pleasure. Moreover it besought that the chiefs who were sprinkled with a part of the water might return with the heads of their enemies, which is the greatest and only measure of their victory" (Bennett 1975, 83).

Then, Laudonnière wrote, Saturiba "embarked and went forward with such speed in his boats that by two hours before sunset on the next day he had arrived in the enemy land" (Bennett 1975, 85), about ten leagues from the village. Once ashore, Saturiba set up a council of war, which decided that five of the chiefs and their warriors would move upriver and wait near the village. Meanwhile, Saturiba and the remaining half of the forces would approach the village by land, and at daybreak the two forces would mount a coordinated attack. The plan worked well enough for the Timucuans to take many scalps, along with twenty-four prisoners. Safely back at the boats, Saturiba ordered the chanting of praises to the sun, which the Indians credited with their victory. At Chief Omoloa's village they divided the prisoners, thirteen of them to Saturiba. The Indian king arrived in triumph at his home near the mouth of the River of May, where he displayed outside his door all the enemy scalps, crowned with magnolia leaves. According to Timucuan custom, the Indians first lamented the men injured or killed in battle, then celebrated and danced for the victory.

In the aftermath of this triumph, Laudonnière proposed to Saturiba that the prisoners be returned to Outina to strengthen a French alliance with that Indian king (Bennett 1975, 86). Coming on the heels of the earlier French refusal to fight with him against his enemies, this new plan must have enraged Saturiba. At any rate, he declined Laudonnière's suggestion. The Frenchman countered with a threat to take the prisoners by force, a threat he could back up with superior weaponry. Saturiba had no real choice. Once the prisoners had been returned to Outina, Laudonnière sprung the next part of his plan: to bring Outina and Saturiba into an undefeatable alliance. Saturiba acquiesced for the moment, sending the French a message in which he not only agreed to their proposal but assured them a continued supply of foodstuffs from his subjects.

Saturiba officiating at a ceremony of war. Engraving by Jacques Le Moyne De Morgues in his *Brevis Narratio* (Frankfurt: de Bry, 1591).

Predictably, Laudonnière's men met with a warm reception when they returned the prisoners to Outina, further demonstrating their good faith by joining him in combat against another chief. They returned to La Caroline with gifts of silver and gold from the Thimogona king along with a pledge to furnish braves any time the French might need them. Although Saturiba indicated his approval of these events when they were explained to him, succeeding events suggest that he remained skeptical.

On 29 August 1564 a great shaft of lightning ignited the marshes near the Indians' home at the mouth of the River of May. Saturiba presumed the fire to be the result of a French cannonade, a misunderstanding seized on by Laudonnière to serve his own end when Saturiba's messengers brought word that their king found the cannonade a strange way for the French to treat Indians who very much wanted to be their allies. Laudonnière recorded:

I spoke expediently as to what I thought of the matter at that time, responding to the Indians with a happy countenance and saying that what they had told me of the obedience of their chief was very agreeable with me because previously he had not behaved himself in that way toward me, especially when I had told him to send me the prisoners that he detained of the great Olata Ouae Outina, even though he . . . counted them unimportant. I told him that this was the principal reason why I had sent the cannonade, and not that I had wanted to reach his house, as I could easily have done that if I had wanted to do so. I said that I had been content to fire just halfway down the course to let him know of my power. I assured him that if he continued in his good behavior, my men would not be shooting at him in the future and I would be his loyal defender against his greatest enemies.

The Indians were content with this response and returned to reassure their chief who, notwithstanding this reassurance, kept away from his home and at a distance of about twenty-five leagues for a period of about two months. (Bennett 1975, 89–90)

Not six months later, however, in January 1565, Saturiba was making new overtures to Laudonnière, demanding that the French soldiers oppose Outina (Bennett 1975, 91, 112). "He pled with me," Laudonnière wrote, "by means of other kings, his allies, who for three or four weeks sent messengers to me for this purpose. But I would not consent that they make war upon Outina. Instead, I endeavored to make them friends. So Satouriona and his allies agreed to await what I would finally say" (Bennett 1975, 112). Apparently blind to his own ambiguous dealings with the Indians, the Frenchman, too, was having problems with trust, as a comment written just previous to this report shows: "I did not trust them myself because I had discovered a thousand of their ruses and tricks, from actual experience as well as from the teachings of modern history" (Bennett 1975, 113).

In spite of their weaponry and belief in their own superiority, the French had a critical weak point. Because the colonists were to have been supplied with foodstuffs from France rather than grow their own crops, and because the only resupply from France had come early in September 1564, by early spring 1565 the colony had become almost entirely dependent on trade with the Indians for food. Saturiba's enthusiasm for trading with the French had been diminished not only by Laudonnière's reluctance to fight Outina but also by the paucity of trade goods remaining to the French and by a shortage of foodstuffs among the Indians themselves. Even before the Indians could reap the early Florida harvest late in the spring of 1565, however, all of Laudonnière's concern was for his fellow Frenchmen. He wrote:

> For practically nothing they obtained from us every bit of merchandise which remained. To make things worse, fearing to be captured by us and seeing that we had spent everything we had, they would not come within gunshot range from our fort. At that distance they brought their fish in their little boats; and there our soldiers were forced to go. Oftentimes I saw our Frenchmen give the very shirts off their backs to obtain one fish. If at any time they remonstrated with the savages about excessive prices, these villains would answer brusquely, "If you value your merchandise so greatly, eat it, and we will eat our fish." Then they would break into laughter and mock us in derision. (Bennett 1975, 124)

Laudonnière turned his wits to getting food for the colonists. When a French detachment sent to help Outina subdue a vassal chief was tricked into fighting Outina's enemies instead, Laudonnière captured the Thimogona king and held him at the fort to be ransomed for food supplies. In short order Saturiba and other Indian leaders turned up at the fort offering a steady supply of food from their early summer harvests in return for the death of Outina. At this juncture Laudonnière described Saturiba as "a steeled and able man, very experienced in negotiations." Finally, even Saturiba saw his efforts were in vain and stopped sending Laudonnière "corn and acorns . . . ambassadors and foodstuffs," and Outina was returned to his own village in exchange for food (Bennett 1975, 129). As the French set out to return to La Caroline, however, their party was ambushed and most of the provisions stolen.

Alert to every gastronomic opportunity, Laudonnière sent a group of his men to investigate rumors that Athore, one of

Saturiba's sons, was visiting on the Satilla River to feast and socialize with the Indian maidens known to be "the prettiest girls and women of the countryside." The French were evidently welcomed by the celebrants, and after they "were given as good a time as could be arranged," Laudonnière reported, "the barques were quickly loaded with corn" (Bennett 1975, 140).

Such interludes of plenty were rare. Famine and failure created great dissension among the colonists, who were not only wracked by hunger but disappointed in their expectations of personal treasure, and several mutinies occurred.

The mutineers' departure did little to improve the spirits of the remaining colonists, who decided by 1 August 1565 to return to France and set about fitting up vessels for the voyage. While their preparations were under way, Captain John Hawkins of England visited La Caroline and provided the French with adequate supplies for their journey home (Bennett 1975, 141–45), but on 28 August, to the colonists' great joy, Jean Ribault arrived from France with reinforcements and supplies. Saturiba and his subjects joined in welcoming the red-bearded Ribault, who had erected the marble pillar on their land in 1562.

The celebration was short lived. Early in September a large Spanish expedition led by Pedro Menéndez de Avilés captured the French fort and executed most of the colonists. King Philip II of Spain justified the takeover on the grounds that Spain had prior claim to the territory and that religious heresy had to be wiped out. Near the trees where the Frenchmen were hanged, Menéndez had a placard placed which read, "I do this not as to Frenchmen but as to Lutherans" (Bennett 1968, 221). Also put to death were two groups of shipwrecked Frenchmen, Ribault among them, who pursued the Spanish battleships and lost their own ships in a hurricane. Laudonnière escaped and made his way back to France, where he reported to Charles IX the tragic results of his efforts to establish a Huguenot colony on the River of May.

The Spaniards gave the name San Mateo to both the river and the old French fort and made their principal base at St. Augustine, twenty-seven miles south. Saturiba did not welcome them as he had the French. Perhaps he resented the massacre of his sometime allies, perhaps in view of the Spanish habit of taking Indians as slaves he grew nostalgic for the comparatively democratic Laudonnière. Whatever his motives, the Indian king and his Timucuans declared war on the Spanish.

Saturiba's tactics made the Indians more often than not the victors in their battles with the Spaniards. When the smoke and flash of a firing arquebus revealed the soldiers' position, the Indians showered them with arrows from their hiding places in the tall grasses and palmettos. The Spaniards' counterstrategy of breaking the spent arrows proved futile. On one occasion, one of Saturiba's vassal chiefs persuaded Spaniards visiting his village to prove their friendship by extinguishing the fuses of their weapons. When they complied, the chief promptly executed his new friends. In another incident, on 28 September 1566, Father Pedro Martínez, a Jesuit missionary en route to St. Augustine to work among the Indians, landed by mistake on Cumberland Island. As he attempted to make his way south to St. Augustine, he was killed by some of his intended converts, subjects of Saturiba (Lowery 1959, 2:271, 272).

If official Spanish policy proved difficult for Saturiba to live with, even worse were the actions of Spanish mutineers, disillusioned like the French before them by the scarcity of food and the lack of easy wealth. Planning to abandon the San Mateo fort, they killed several Indians to incite Saturiba against the settlement as they left it. In retaliation, the Indian king killed the two Spanish messengers sent from the remaining garrison to alert St. Augustine to the mutiny and had their hearts ceremonially removed (Lowery 1959, 2:242). Even the nonmutinous Spaniards persisted in pillaging Saturiba's villages and enslaving some of his Indians, in defiance of a royal decree against Indian slavery.

After Menéndez's forces had managed to kill several of Saturiba's vassal chiefs, taking a number of prisoners, the Spanish leader thought the time might be ripe for a peace parley. Although he and Saturiba were able to agree on a time and place to meet on the riverbank, once there Menéndez refused to come ashore from his rowboat and Saturiba refused to talk until he did. Fearing a trap, Menéndez had himself rowed back to San Mateo and soon after attacked the Indians again with no decisive outcome (Lowery 1959, 2:283). Menéndez also took the opportunity to aid Outina in his continuing war against Saturiba, sending eighty soldiers under Pedro de Andrada to burn the village of one of Saturiba's vassals. Their victory proved hollow. Saturiba's warriors lay in wait for the victors on their return to St. Augustine and slew Andrada and a large portion of his company (Lowery 1959, 2:294).[5]

Back in France, where emotions still ran high over the Fort Caroline massacre, Dominique de Gourgues, a Catholic and a man of substance and courage, financed an expedition of revenge. He set sail from Bordeaux on 2 August 1567 with 180 men in three vessels, ostensibly headed for Africa to fight the Portuguese black colony there. The expedition had two encounters in Africa before sailing for Florida. Not until the ships were off Cape San Antonio, Cuba, did Gourgues announce to his crew their true objective: the conquest of Spanish San Mateo, in retaliation for the 1565 massacre of the French (Lowery 1959, 2:314–36).

As the Gourgues expedition sailed toward Florida, Estéban de las Alas, commander at St. Augustine in Menéndez's absence, early in 1568 carried out Menéndez's urgent instructions to build two blockhouses at the mouth of the San Mateo River, Fort San Estéban on the south bank and Fort San Gabriel on the north (Roncière 1928, 123). On 31 March, soon after the blockhouses were completed, four hundred of Saturiba's warriors attacked Fort San Mateo. Entering by a breach in the palisades, they killed one soldier and severely wounded Castellon, the fort's commander (Lowery 1959, 2:297).

Only a few weeks later, in mid-April, Gourgues landed at Cumberland Island, where eighteen months earlier Indians

5. See also *Dépeches de Fourquevaux, ambassaodeur de roi Charles IX en Espagne (1565–72)*, ed. C. Douais (Paris, 1896), 295, and Edward W. Lawson, trans. and ed., "Letters of Pedro Menéndez de Avilés and Other Documents," typescript, Bennett Collection, 328. The Spanish letter of 6 August 1567 is from Chaplain Francisco López de Mendoza to Pedro Menéndez; he wrote, "About twelve or fifteen days ago Captain Pedro de Andrada left here on account of Outina and carried in his company eight soldiers to make war on Saturiba." Andrada was not identified by name in the French letter.

had murdered Father Martínez. Gourgues, too, was met by a host of Indians, among them Saturiba and some of his vassal kings. When Saturiba demanded clear assurances that Gourgues and his company were the Indians' pledged French allies, a trumpeter who had been among the French at Fort Caroline came forward and spoke to him. Saturiba remained skeptical. "If you are truly the French you say you are," he challenged, "sing for us the psalms they sang in the times of Laudonnière and Jean Ribault" (*Histoire mémorable* 1568, 4).[6] When the Frenchmen sang the Forty-third, Fiftieth, and Ninety-first Psalms, according to an account many historians credit to Gourgues himself, Saturiba was convinced and launched into a catalogue of the sins the Spanish had visited upon the Indians.

He insisted that "since the Spaniards had captured the fort built by the French, Florida had never had one good day, that the Spaniards had continually made war upon them, had driven them from their houses, cut their maize, ravished their wives, carried away their daughters, and killed their little children" (Bennett 1968, 210). He went on to assure Gourgues that "although he and the other Kings had suffered all these ills on account of the friendship they had entered into with the French by whom the land had first been inhabited, yet they had never ceased to love the French because of the good treatment they had received from them when they commanded there" (Bennett 1968, 210).

Captain Gourgues recognized an opportunity when one presented itself. "In order to strike the iron while it was hot, he said to [the Indians], 'Verily, if we wanted to make war, it would have to be at once. How much time would it take you to assemble your men ready to march?'" Saturiba assured him that the kings and their subjects could reassemble at Cumberland Island in three days. Gourgues then warned the kings to keep their preparations secret from the Spaniards. "Have no fear," they replied, "we wish them more harm than you do" (Bennett 1968, 210, 212).

As proof of his dedication to the new alliance, Saturiba told

6. The Fort Caroline National Memorial files contain a facsimile of *Histoire mémorable*. Clement Marot and Theodore de Besze published in rhyme *Les Psaumes de David* in Geneva in 1560 and in Paris in 1561 (Roncière 1928).

Gourgues, "I will give you my only son, and that one of my wives whom I love the most, so that you may know that we are not liars nor traitors, as are these Spaniards who deceive us always, and never do anything of what they promise us" (Bennett 1968, 213).[7] The Gourgues manuscript goes on to report that "the King's son was entirely naked, as were also all the other men. The King's wife was clothed in moss, and was about eighteen. They remained three days on board Captain Gourgues' vessels, awaiting the return of those who had gone to reconnoiter the fort" (Bennett 1968, 213).

Once the combined Indian and French forces had assembled, "before departing, the savages brewed a certain beverage called by them cassine, which they are accustomed to drink when they go to fight in a place where there is danger. The beverage, made from a certain herb and drunk very hot, preserves them from hunger and thirst for the space of twenty-four hours. They presented some of it first to Captain Gourgues, who pretended to drink it, but did not swallow any thereof. Then King Saturiba took some, and after him all the others, each according to his rank. That done, with many ceremonies, they all raised their hand, and swore and promised that they would do their duty of fighting well, and would not forsake Captain Gourgues" (Bennett 1968, 214).

On 24 April 1568, the allied forces surprised Fort San Gabriel's sixty defenders at their noonday meal. The same day, the Indians swam the river and the French crossed in a pinnace to storm Fort San Estéban, killing most of the garrison and taking fifteen prisoners. The French returned to Alimacany on the north shore[8] to prepare for their attack on San Mateo and learned from a captured Spanish spy that the San Mateo garrison was greatly overestimating the strength of the French forces. On 27 April, when Gourgues advanced on the former French fort, most of its 120 defenders fled in disarray. In a poetic gesture, Gourgues hung his Spanish captives "to the same trees where they had hanged the Frenchmen" and "had inscribed on a pine tablet with a hot iron: 'I

7. The manuscript's mistaken reference to Saturiba's "only son" may be interpreted as his only still dependent son, because another adult son, Athore, was present during this exchange.
8. Today, Fort George Island.

Saturiba, from André Thevêt's *Les vrais Pourtraits et vies des hommes* (Paris, 1584).

do this not as to Spaniards, nor as to Marannos [converted Jews], but as to traitors, robbers, and murderers'" (Bennett 1968, 221).

Captain Gourgues led his victorious forces back to Cumberland Island, where, as he prepared to set sail for France, he promised Saturiba and his other Indian allies to return soon. The French welcomed Gourgues as a hero, although the government muted its approval to head off the possibility of war with Spain. He did not keep his promise to return to the River of May. Two hundred and twenty-five years would pass before the French flag would again fly over Florida.[9]

Although the Timucuans carried on their opposition to the Spanish, after his alliance with Gourgues no details have come to light of the activities of their king, the clever and charismatic Saturiba.

9. The flag of the Republic of France flew over northeastern Florida from 1793 to 1795 (Bennett 1970, 60). See also the more detailed study in Bennett 1982.

TWO

~~~~~~

Nicolas Barré
and Jean Ribault

GEOGRAPHER NICOLAS BARRÉ AND EXPEDI-
tion commander Jean Ribault first dropped anchor in Florida's
waters on 30 April 1562. Their three-masted ships had sailed
from Dieppe, France, nearly three months earlier. Exploring
north along the Florida coast, the French came ashore a second time at the river the Indians there called the Welaka and
renamed it the River of May to commemorate their landing
date. Although their ships moved on after a few days, Barré
and Ribault would return to the River of May three years later
with hundreds of colonists to replenish and strengthen La Caroline, the fledgling French Huguenot settlement established
by then near the river's mouth. Defending that settlement
against a Spanish attack, the two would die forty miles from
the river they had named and nearly four thousand miles from
their homeland.

Barré is a common surname in France's Loire Valley and
the name of a village near Amboise on the Loire. It has long
been assumed that Nicolas Barré came from that area (Cumming 1963, 30), but little is known about his early life.
Based on the considerable skills he evidenced as an adult, a
good part of his early years must have been spent studying
the natural world.

Jean Ribault's roots were in the seaport town of Dieppe. A

Calvinist, in his early adulthood he was among the leaders in France's religious wars. His knowledge of navigation had several times put him in the employ of Henry VIII and Edward VI of England (Bennett 1975, xiii),[1] and he had represented French interests in important negotiations with England and Scotland (Connor 1927, 4).

Barré first sailed to the New World as pilot of an expedition in the mid-1550s to establish a settlement in lands claimed by Portugal, beside a harbor that today is overlooked by the city of Rio de Janeiro. France's Henry II authorized the project as a haven for Huguenots (French Protestants) in "Antarctic France" under the leadership of Nicolas Durand, Sieur de Villegaignon. Villegaignon had a distinguished military record: he fought for France in Algiers in 1541, commanded the galleys that brought Mary Stuart safely from Scotland in 1548, and soon thereafter fought against the Turks in Malta (Grant 1907, 206). Although a staunch Catholic, Villegaignon's dream of exploring the New World had led him to suggest the colony to Gaspard de Coligny, a powerful figure in the French court. Coligny in turn persuaded Henry II to allow the trip, stressing the possibilities of expanding France's realm and enriching her treasury.

The voyage got off to a slow start. In a letter dated 1 February 1556, Barré described how the expedition's two-masted Dutch vessel and two tall ships set out from Le Havre on 12 July 1555 only to be forced back to Dieppe by a storm. The townspeople of Dieppe, he wrote, "were present in such great numbers to haul on the hawsers and cables that with their help we entered the harbor" despite the shallow waters. The aborted voyage nevertheless had its casualties, Barré observed: "Several of our gentlemen found that they had seen enough of the sea, thereby fulfilling the saying: 'He looked at the sea, and fled' " (Grant 1907, 149; Gaffarel 1878, 179). When, according to Barré, God had "calmed the anger of the sea and fury of the sky," the small fleet sailed again from Dieppe on 14 August, Villegaignon aboard one of the tall ships and Barré piloting the other, the *Vice Admiral*.

1. For information about Ribault before 1562, see Roncière 1923 (3:453, 558) and Gaffarel 1875 (13).

In the Canary Islands off the coast of Africa, Barré commented upon sighting Tenerife's Mount Atlas that geographers of the time believed this mountain to be the source of the name of the Atlantic Ocean. The expedition exchanged a few rounds with Spanish settlers on Tenerife, then sailed away into another period of bad winds. During the inclement weather, the ailing Villegaignon moved to the *Vice Admiral* for better care.

Near the equator Barré reported finding "so great a number of fish of such diverse species that sometimes we thought we would run aground on them"—porpoises, whales, bonito, and flying fish that flew "in troops like the starlings in our country." Soon after, the drinking water grew foul, and the winds again turned unfavorable. "In these great perplexities, and almost without hope," Barré wrote, "the Lord God sent us a southwest wind" which sped them on to the shores of South America. On 10 November 1555, after nearly three months at sea, the colonists landed at the River of Ganabara in Brazil "singing praises and giving thanks to the Lord" (Grant 1907, 155; Gaffarel 1878, 182). The Huguenots built their settlement on an island at the river's mouth and named it Fort Coligny.

Fort Coligny's greatest handicap proved to be its erratic and tyrannical leader, Villegaignon, a devout Catholic at the head of a Protestant settlement. He turned on the Huguenot clergymen he had secured for the colony, first quarreling with them on issues of heresy, finally exiling and even executing some Huguenots who refused to accept his views of Catholic traditions and scriptural interpretations. Nicolas Barré, a Huguenot himself, as well as Villegaignon's right-hand man and the colony's secretary, made peace where he could.

As destructive as they were, clashes of religious belief were not the colonists' only problem. Hostile Portuguese and unfriendly Indians were never far away. Food was scarce. The men's hoped-for riches proved illusory. Of the more than three hundred colonists, only five were women, and Villegaignon forbade the men to socialize with Indian women. Mutiny was in the air. On 25 May 1556, Barré wrote that he had learned from the Scot guarding Villegaignon of a plot to kill Villegaignon, Barré, and other leaders. Barré had the mutineers put in chains (Grant 1907, 160).

Historians believe that Nicolas Barré returned to France with Villegaignon two years later, in 1558, after three years of mutinies, banishments, executions, and religious dissension at Fort Coligny. Villegaignon turned the colony's leadership over to his nephew Bois-Lecomte. On 15 March 1560, the settlement fell to the Portuguese, who claimed the area by right of previous settlement and by papal decree (Smith 1891, 3:200).

The fall of Fort Coligny in South America followed the next year by a Spanish order discouraging Spanish settlement in the north lent force to Gaspard de Coligny's advice to create a new Huguenot settlement on the North Atlantic coast. Charles IX had succeeded to the throne of France in 1560. Now his mother, Catherine de Medici, decided in 1562 that the twelve-year-old king would take Coligny's advice and send an expedition to New France or Terre de Bretons, as she called Spanish Florida (Lowery 1959, 2:300). To assist in the project, she turned to three men: Jean Ribault, Nicolas Barré, and René Laudonnière.[2] The three longtime acquaintances shared not only a devotion to the reformed religion of John Calvin but also diplomatic and navigational skills. Laudonnière had commanded important voyages for France in the eastern hemisphere (Bennett 1964, 9). Barré was especially well qualified, having recent firsthand knowledge of the New World's natives and resources.

On 16 February 1562, a fleet of three ships—two Dutch three-masters and a large sloop, along with two small boats carried aboard—set out from Dieppe for New France. Jean Ribault was fleet commander, René Laudonnière second in command, and Nicolas Barré chief geographer and cartographer.

The expedition reached Florida on 30 April and spent a few days in the vicinity of present-day St. Augustine and Jacksonville, long enough to rechristen the river there the River of

2. Like Barré's, Laudonnière's ancestral home was in the Loire Valley, near Nantes. The ruins of Laudonnière's chateau lie today near the chateau of the Marquis de Gaulaine, a collateral descendant.

Port Royal, where Nicolas Barré governed Charlesfort in 1563. Engraving by Jacques Le Moyne De Morgues in his *Brevis Narratio* (Frankfurt: de Bry, 1591).

May and to befriend the Timucuans and their king, Saturiba. As they sailed farther north, Ribault directed Barré to map every river, island, and other geographical feature of the coastline they passed, and the two men gave them all names. A spot on a sheltered island off the coast of present-day South Carolina they named Port Royal, and here Ribault decided a settlement should be built.

To recruit volunteer colonists, Ribault appealed first to the men's honor, loyalty to the king, and ambition.

> I think all of you know that our enterprise is of great importance and greatly desired by our young king. Therefore, my friends, desiring both your honor and your welfare, I want to explain to you how great an honor it will be for those of you who, with valor and true courage will test in our first exploration the virtues and assets of this new land. . . . You being descended from average stock, few or none of your parents have

ever made a profession of arms nor have been found among the great estates. As for myself, from my early years I applied all of my industry to follow the royal family and have hazarded my life in many dangers for the service of my king. Without this I could never have attained this position of leadership. (Bennett 1975, 32)

After pointing to various historical figures who had reaped honor and renown through service to their country, Ribault played his trump card, immortality: "These memorable examples should persuade you to stay here. Remember that for this you will always be revered as those who were first to live in this strange land. I beg you then to discuss it among yourselves and to open your minds freely to me. I promise you to bring your names so forcefully to the ears of the king and the princes that your fame shall hereafter shine inextinguishably in the heart of France" (Bennett 1975, 34).

Among the thirty or so men who volunteered to settle Port Royal were Nicolas Barré, in whom Ribault felt great confidence, and Albert de la Pierrea, a man of untested leadership abilities, who was the first to volunteer and who was elected governor (Connor 1927, 97; Sparks 1845, 7:27). Ribault led the volunteers on an exploratory foray to pick the best site for a fort. He assigned Laudonnière to build it on the shore of a little island inside the mouth of Port Royal, which is the mouth of Broad River.[3] The small fort, only 102 by 83 feet, would be named Charlesfort in honor of the king (Bennett 1975, xiv, 35).

On 11 June 1562, Ribault and Laudonnière, promising to return with supplies in six months, sailed for France with most of the expedition's members. However, when Ribault arrived in France on 20 July, he joined the Protestants of Dieppe, who with the help of English reinforcements were fighting Catholic royal troops. When the Protestant forces capitulated to the French government on 20 October, Ribault fled to England. The next year Rouland Hall, a London publishing house, distributed Ribault's chronicle of the 1562 expedition, *The Whole & True Discouerye of Terra Florida*.

When the publication came to the attention of Queen

3. Archeologists have not yet pinpointed the site of the fort.

Elizabeth, she offered Ribault the opportunity to rescue the Charlesfort colonists. The plan went awry when Ribault's proposed partner in the venture, Thomas Stukeley, clandestinely offered to sabotage it to protect Spanish interests. Apparently learning of Stukeley's betrayal, Ribault attempted to escape from England but was caught by Elizabeth's troops and imprisoned in the Tower of London in June 1563.

At Charlesfort, famine, dissension, and the accidental burning of the fort had created strong sentiment for returning to France (Connor 1927, 8; Lowery 1959, 2:41–44; Folmer 1953, 81). The colonists had searched for ore but had grown no crops, subsisting mostly on the largesse of friendly Indians. Although Barré had tried to maintain order, Captain Albert de la Pierrea proved to be an erratic and emotional leader. For unknown or insufficient reasons, he had, for example, hung the drummer and banished a colonist named Larcher. Finally, one of the men killed Captain Pierrea in self-defense, and Nicolas Barré was elected the new governor.

Barré was "a man worthy of command," Laudonnière would later report to Charles IX. "He knew so well how to carry out his responsibilities that rancor and dissension ended among [the colonists] and they lived peacefully among themselves" (Bennett 1975, 47). But even Barré could not produce food out of thin air. By this time the neighboring Indians were experiencing a severe food shortage themselves, and the promised resupply from France had not arrived. The colonists decided to build a boat to return to their homes across the Atlantic.

None of the men had any knowledge of boatbuilding, but with Barré's forceful leadership and tactful enlistment of Indian help they persevered. Laudonnière described part of the construction process: "Our Frenchmen sought by every possible means to get resin in the woods. They cut the bark of the pines and brought out enough to cover the boat. Also to caulk the boat they gathered a kind of moss which grows on trees in this area. They now lacked nothing but the sails, and these they made from their shirts and bedclothes. Several days afterward, the Indians returned to Charlesfort with many ropes, which were found ample to equip the small boat" (Bennett 1975, 48). To build goodwill for the French who would be returning to settle these lands, Barré ordered the men to give the Indians everything of value not needed on the voyage. Early in 1564 the Charlesfort settlers set sail for France, only to become the victims of alternating calms and erratic gusts as their fresh water and food gave out. In three weeks they sailed only twenty-five leagues, perhaps seventy-five miles. They rationed themselves to no more than twelve grains by weight of cornmeal daily per man, and when even the cornmeal was gone they ate their shoes, leather collars, straps, and dried animal skins. Some drank seawater, which swelled their throats and made their guts burn; others drank their own urine. The boat's hull began to burst at the seams, and a tidal wave threw the vessel against a rock. For three days without food or drink, out of sight of land, they simply bailed. Finally, it was suggested that one should die to save the rest. The lot fell to the banished Larcher, whom they killed, dividing his flesh among them and drinking his warm blood. When they at last saw the land of Britain, they collapsed and drifted with the waves until an English vessel rescued the strong among them and took them to the queen, abandoning the weaker to the sea (Bennett 1964, 82).

Barré was among those taken to England, where he was imprisoned. Although France immediately opened a vigorous diplomatic correspondence to secure his prompt release, he remained in prison for nearly a year. In a letter of 1 January 1565, Queen Elizabeth wrote that she had released to the French ambassador a "Monsr. Barry," who was "a companion of Ribaulde being taken in this last warre coming out of Terra florida, whom he [the ambassador] sendeth also unto France at this tyme wt this packett" (Cumming 1963, 31).

Once again Barré signed on with Ribault for an expedition to Florida, this time to relieve Laudonnière at Fort Caroline on the River of May. On 10 May 1565, Ribault's seven-ship fleet set out from Le Havre, carrying more than three hundred men, women, and children to swell the settlement. Their ships anchored at Fort Caroline on 28 August, their arrival somewhat delayed by a reconnoitering of the Florida coast.

Only days later, the Spanish fleet under Pedro Menéndez appeared, bent on reclaiming the colonized land. For two days, Ribault debated with Laudonnière and François Léger de la Grange, his "colonel of troops and director of fortifications"

(Connor 1927, 15), how best to defend the colony.[4] Ribault favored attacking the Spanish at sea, whereas Laudonnière and La Grange urged that, particularly since it was hurricane season, the best strategy was to reinforce Fort Caroline against a Spanish land attack. Barré refereed the discussions until finally La Grange acquiesced. Along with all able-bodied military men from Fort Caroline, he joined Ribault and the fleet, which sailed in pursuit of the Spanish (Connor 1927, 22, 23).

The decision to fight at sea was a mistake. A hurricane destroyed the French fleet. Ribault's ship, the *Trinity*, was wrecked on the beach south of St. Augustine. La Grange drowned clinging to a mast. Barré, Ribault, and all others aboard made it to shore (Connor 1927, 28). Meanwhile, Menéndez and the Spanish fleet landed safely at what is now St. Augustine. He promptly opted to march northward and capture Fort Caroline, there massacring all but a few colonists. Laudonnière, who had remained at the fort because of illness, escaped with others who fled the fort and were rescued by a French ship that had not been with the shipwrecked Ribault task force. Menéndez marched his victorious troops southward to an inlet called barreta de Ribao or Matanzas (Connor 1927, 28, 42).[5] Ribault and his party marched northward to that inlet and there found Menéndez waiting for them.

With some ambiguity in choice of words, Menéndez accepted the French surrender and in a little boat brought Ribault's men across the inlet in small groups. On the north shore, he executed all the Protestants except a few talented workmen and musicians (Lowery 1959, 199).[6]

Barré witnessed the death of Jean Ribault while awaiting his own execution (Thevêt [1575] 1953, 304). As Ribault was

4. Ribault had selected La Grange specifically to advise him in combat situations. According to a spy report he was "a man who has never been to sea" (Archivo de la Real Academia de la Historia, Madrid, 9-30-3, 6271; a transcript translated by Eugene Lyon is available at the Fort Caroline National Memorial).

5. After 1565 the inlet was variously called barreta de Ribao and barreta del Peñón. Now silted in, it lies one league south of Matanzas Inlet.

6. Menéndez's acts must be understood as those of a man not only convinced that Catholicism was the only true faith but also aware that he had no way to handle large numbers of prisoners—men who, after all, had settled land to which Spain claimed prior title.

about to die, he said, "Twenty years more or less are of little account," then chanted the One Hundred Thirty-second Psalm as a dagger thrust killed him (Lowery 1959, 199).[7] The details of Nicolas Barré's death, like those of his early life, remain obscure. Some evidence suggests, however, that his executioner, Menéndez, may have charted his course to Fort Caroline in 1565 from a copy of one of Barré's own maps.[8] Although the original has not been found, Barré certainly drafted a map at Charlesfort after his 1562 voyage with Ribault from the River of May to Port Royal (Cumming 1963, 27). A sixteenth-century tracing of such a map with Spanish notations by a Spanish hand is in Madrid's Naval Museum. It may be that Bishop Quadra, Spanish ambassador to Elizabeth's government, stole a copy from Barré's cell or from Ribault's quarters in the tower. The writing on the tracing and accompanying notes is crude, and the map signature "Parreus" may actually have been inaccurately traced from Barré's signature.

Clandestine copying of documents and maps was common in the sixteenth century, and evidently these tracings and notes were intended to augment Spanish intelligence (Cumming 1963, 29). The copy of Barré's map may have been used by Hernando de Manrique de Rojas, who sailed from Havana in May 1564 to find out about Charlesfort (Cumming 1963, 29, 30). On that voyage Rojas destroyed the remains of the abandoned Port Royal post and carried away the French stone column, a twin to the one at Mayport. And in the final irony, a Spanish copy of Nicolas Barré's 1562 map may have led Menéndez to the site of Barré's own execution.

7. In this psalm, David speaks of seeking and finding a place for God to dwell among men on earth and of receiving God's blessings for the deed.

8. Barré's talents also benefited his own countrymen. André Thevêt, the distinguished sixteenth-century French geographer and cosmographer, became acquainted with Barré on the 1555 expedition to Brazil. "He was my great friend and companion," Thevêt wrote after Barré's death, "whose memory I treasure mostly for our close and unique friendship but also for the knowledge and understanding he gave" of American plants, animals, geography, and anthropology, and of her countrysides and waterways, particularly in Florida ([1575] 1953, 304). After the publication of his *France Antartique* in 1558 and *Cosmographie Universelle* in 1575, Thevêt was named "Cosmographe du Roy" (Legear 1949, 21).

THREE

〰〰〰〰〰〰〰〰〰〰〰〰〰〰〰〰〰〰〰

Francisco Pareja

FRIAR FRANCISCO PAREJA LANDED AT ST. Augustine with nine other Franciscans in the fall of 1595, thirty years after his countryman Pedro Menéndez executed Nicolas Barré and Jean Ribault nearby for being Protestants and French interlopers on Spanish territory. The Franciscans came to convert the Indians to Catholicism, and for the next thirty years Pareja would work with the Timucuans in Spanish Florida from his base mission, San Juan del Puerto, on San Juan Island at the mouth of the river the French had named the River of May and the Spanish called the San Mateo.[1] There he would write "the earliest surviving text in any North American Indian language" (Milanich and Sturtevant 1972, 15), and his mission would become so well known that in time it would give its name to the river—the San Juan.

The zealous beliefs of Pedro Menéndez de Avilés were at least partly responsible for bringing Pareja to Florida. Shortly after overcoming the French in 1565, Menéndez asked Spanish authorities to send missionaries to work among the Indians. He envisioned converting, if not the entire native Indian popu-

1. A century and a half later this island on the north side of the mouth of the St. Johns would be called Fort George, when General James Oglethorpe built Fort Saint George there, probably on a rise on the island's eastern side.

lation of North America, at least the tribes of the eastern seaboard as far north as present-day Virginia. By 1566, Jesuit
brothers had arrived on the scene (Geiger 1937, 34). They met
with less success in North America than they had enjoyed farther south, and on 9 February 1571 Indians murdered several
priests at their mission near today's Fredericksburg, Virginia
(Gannon 1965, 34). When the Jesuits retired from the field the
next year, Menéndez requested Franciscan friars to replace
them. He lived just long enough to see the first Franciscan
contingent of four or five brothers (Gannon 1965, 36) arrive in
1573. Thirteen more Franciscans joined them in 1587 (Geiger
1937, 53, 54). But life in Spanish Florida was hard, and by 1592
only three priests and one lay brother remained (Gannon 1965,
39; Geiger 1937, 58).

A royal cedula of 22 March 1595 ordered up reinforcements— twelve Franciscan brothers, among them Friar Francisco Pareja. Two became ill and did not sail. The ship bearing
the remaining ten approached the Florida coast in the fall of
1595, surviving the buffeting of a storm only to run aground
in heavy seas within view of the harbor at San Agustín. One
of the friars, Father Escobedo, described the pilot's reaction:
He first cried out to God, then "with the tenseness showing
in his face, for he knew that no one could swim ashore, he
turned to the friars and requested their prayers." Next, the
priest wrote, "a wonderful event occurred which saved our
vessel from destruction and allowed us to resume the voyage
to San Agustín. While the friars were praying for aid, the vessel shifted its position and drifting into deeper water resumed
the journey. When the ship had passed into the harbor of the
port called San Agustín, everyone gave thanks to the Lord for
having rescued them from disaster and allowing them to go
free" (Covington 1963, 20, 21).

They landed on 23 September 1595 (Geiger 1937, 64).
Among his descriptions of the newly arriving friars, Father
Escobedo wrote that Francisco Pareja was "such a sincere,
modest and quiet person that he was considered a virtual
saint. He always made himself available to the most abandoned, praying for them, and while telling them about the
method to obtain grace, he urged the sinners to cast aside

their bad habits" (Covington 1963, 20). A well-educated man of scholarly bent, Pareja came to Florida from Auñón in the Spanish province of Castille.

After a brief period of rest at the San Agustín friary, Pareja and the other new arrivals set out for their respective mission assignments, ceremonially escorted by Governor Domingo Martínez de Avendaño and an infantry detachment in a show of royal support for the clergy (Geiger 1937, 65). Pareja's first assignment was to the San Pedro mission on Cumberland Island, where in 1566 Indians had murdered Father Martínez. On 24 November, Governor Avendaño died there while visiting Pareja. His replacement, appointed by Philip II, was Mendez de Canzo (Gerónimo de Oré 1936, 71; Lanning 1935, 70). Pareja became the Indians' advocate almost immediately, making the first move in a campaign against the Spanish colonial government that he would wage throughout his career. Governor Canzo, Pareja wrote the king, failed to give adequate support to the mission work at San Pedro as well as elsewhere in Spanish Florida. The crux of the problem was the fixed royal subsidy for all Florida expenditures, missionary and military. However much the governor may have appreciated the priests' work, more friars meant less pay for soldiers. Competition between these two systems was a fact of colonial life (Geiger 1937, 67).[2]

Within several months, Pareja was given primary responsibility for the San Juan del Puerto mission on the western shore of San Juan Island (Gerónimo de Oré 1936, 57, 143). San Pedro and San Juan formed the southern terminus of the Indian mission district that stretched along the coast from the Río San Mateo north to South Carolina. The district was called Guale, or sometimes Río Salado (Salt River) for its brackish inland passage and to distinguish it from the neighboring Agua Dulce, the Sweet Water (or Fresh Water) district of the Río San Mateo valley. San Agustín lay in the Timucuan mission district (Geiger 1937, 146).

From San Juan, Friar Pareja set off on long journeys to

2. By 1600, the governor could fill only 250 of his alloted quota of 300 spaces for soldiers; the remainder went to friars, pilots, and sailors.

Sixteenth-century majolica fragment showing a priest. Sherd was found at the site of the San Juan del Puerto mission. Courtesy Florida Division of Historical Resources.

carry Catholicism to the Indians. Usually alone and barefoot, he confronted the dangers of a subtropical wilderness, a land of islands, streams, marshes, and lakes, of panthers, bears, and alligators, poisonous moccasins, rattlesnakes, and coral snakes, deadly spiders, scorpions, and fever-bearing mosquitoes. Hostile Indians, both backsliders from the faith and the unconverted, had ample practice in torture and murder, as well as the barbarous example of some of their Spanish conquerors. "In the beginning," wrote Pareja's superior, Father Luis Gerónimo de Oré, "the Indians offered him many affronts but he overcame them all with much patience and perseverance by abiding in their midst, teaching them the law of Christ and defending them from the molestation of the Spanish soldiers. By these deeds and through the power of his example, which he always gave, he overcame the harshness and cruelty of the Indians, changing them from wolves to sheep" (1936, 69).

Not all the Indians, however. In 1597, many Indians of the Guale mission district rebelled. Their primary grievance was the friars' insistence that the Indians practice monogamy (Geiger 1937, 88), and the precipitating event occurred in Tolomato, on the mainland opposite Sapelo Island (which is just north of the mouth of the Altamaha River in McIntosh County, Georgia). There, Father Corpa publicly reprimanded Juanillo, heir apparent to the Tolomato chiefdom, for having more than one wife. As Father Corpa saw it, this circumstance threw into doubt Juanillo's rights to property and the chiefdom (Geiger 1937, 88). On 13 September, Juanillo and some of his pagan supporters killed Father Corpa with a stone hatchet as he knelt at morning prayer. They exhibited the friar's head on the end of a lance at the village landing and buried his body where they thought the Christians could not find it. The community then reinstituted the practices of polygamy and exchanging wives (Geiger 1937, 89). Juanillo soon thereafter pled with a gathering of neighboring Guale chiefs to restore the old order:

> Since the punishment for killing one friar must be equally severe as for killing all, let us restore our [ancient] liberty of which these friars deprive us. They give us promises of good things which they themselves have not seen but for which they hold out hope. We who are called Christians, experience only hindrances and vexations. They take away from us our women, allowing us but one, and that in perpetuity, forbidding us to exchange them for others. They prohibit us from having our dances, banquets, feasts, celebrations, games and wars, in order that, being deprived of these, we might lose our ancient valor and skill, which we have inherited from our ancestors. They persecute our old men, calling them wizards. They are not satisfied with our labor for they hinder us from performing it on certain days. Even when we are willing to do all they tell us, they remain unsatisfied. All they do, is to reprimand us, treat us in an injurious manner, oppress us, preach to us and call us bad Christians. They deprive us of every vestige of happiness which our ancestors obtained for us, in exchange for which they hold out the hope of joys of Heaven. In this deceitful manner, they subject us, holding us bound to their wills. What have we to hope for except to become slaves? If we kill them all now, we will throw off this intolerable yoke without delay. The governor will perceive our valor and will be forced to treat us well, in the event that he should get the better of us. (Geiger 1937, 90)

Juanillo's arguments were persuasive. Not long afterward, Indians murdered Father Auñón and Brother Antonio, a lay brother, at their mission on Guale Island, and at the Ospo mission on Jekyll Island, Father Francisco de Avila was seriously wounded (Gerónimo de Oré 1936, 85). The Indians took Avila, bloody and untended, to the village of Ufulague, then to Tulafina, where they placed him next to a cross and started a fire near him to torture him in his nakedness. They abandoned a plan to burn him to death, sparing him because of his good deeds and his value in a possible exchange for an Indian held at San Agustín (Geiger 1937, 88).[3] In the meantime, they kept him enslaved, forced him to watch them mock Christian rites, and tempted him to repudiate his chastity vows by sending a beautiful maiden to prepare a bed and meal for him. With fervent prayer Avila resisted and reported that "in order to safeguard myself from all this, I fled to the woods where I remained for four days. . . ; since then they never spoke to me of such things." After about ten months, he was freed in exchange for the Indian hostage (Geiger 1937, 110).

Indians attacked a fifth religious, Father Francisco de Verascola, as he returned to his mission at Asao following a visit with his brothers at San Agustín. On the pretense of welcoming him, they murdered him instead (Geiger 1937, 99).

The most important target of the rebellion was Father Pareja, the religious leader of the area. The Indians planned his murder for 4 October 1597, the feast of St. Francis, when Pareja would be officiating at ceremonies at San Pedro on Cumberland Island. In the festive atmosphere, the Indians reasoned, they would catch the Christians off guard. Twenty-three canoes crowded with hostile warriors drew up at San Pedro, apparently not intimidated by the Spanish brigantine anchored in the harbor (Geiger 1937, 100). Indians from two canoes attacked the outlying hut of a Christian Indian, Antonio López, seriously injuring his father-in-law, Juesep. López's war cry alerted the mission village.

3. Guale Island is now St. Catherine's Island; it lies between the mouths of the Medway and South Newport rivers, dominating the coastline of Liberty County, Georgia. Jekyll Island lies to the south, off the southern coast of Georgia.

Father Pareja heard the alarm from the door of the San Pedro church and dispatched a messenger to Father Chozas's ministry, Puturiba, at the north end of the island. Then Pareja went to the wounded Juesep to hear his confession. Meanwhile, the village's Christian Indians had rallied under the leadership of Don Juan, their chief, to protect Father Pareja and their own families and to prevent the hostile Indians from burning their palmetto huts and their sturdy timber and mud chapel. So fierce was their enthusiasm for the fray that they soon drove off their attackers, minus one canoe and its occupants. The rebels retreated north up the inland passage, and at Puturiba they threatened Father Chozas, who carried on with his mass honoring St. Francis. Shouting insults from their canoes, the warriors pushed northward without landing. Father Chozas hurried down the island to San Pedro, where he and Father Pareja sent off a report to Governor Canzo by way of the soldiers on the brigantine.

The governor received their report on 7 October, began preparations to punish the Indians, and by the eighteenth arrived at San Pedro with his troops to gather information from Father Pareja. Three days later, Canzo and 150 soldiers moved north to engage the Indians of Guale in battle, meeting with heavy resistance at Ospo on 24 October but routing the Indians soon after their first volley of arrows. As the Spaniards moved north, they found every village abandoned by the Indians retreating ahead of them. Although the soldiers burned each village they passed through, the Indians avoided further combat (Geiger 1937, 103; Covington 1963, 41). Their failure to kill Father Pareja had evidently dampened their enthusiasm.

In the aftermath of the rebellion, Governor Canzo and his troops returned on 11 November to San Pedro, where Canzo conducted a parley with the Indian leaders in the mission church. Don Juan, the Christian chief of the mission town, agreed to move to a safer location, the region of Pareja's San Juan del Puerto. Pareja, Chozas, and several other missionaries went to San Agustín to testify about the revolt. Also questioned were a number of captured Indians, one of whom Canzo put to the rack. Upon his admission that he was present at Father Rodriguez's death, the Indian was hanged on 29 July 1598 (Geiger 1937, 115). In retaliation for the rebellion, Canzo authorized the enslavement of the Guale Indians; the authorization was reversed by the government in Spain, and the slaves were freed and sent back to Guale.

Although most of the Indians of Guale eventually sought peace with the Spanish authorities, at Tolomato, Juanillo and his father, Francisco, remained hostile, and the Spanish reserved the right to punish them (Geiger 1937, 119). In 1601, both were finally killed in a battle with coastal Indians who had been incited to fight by the Spanish authorities. Once Juanillo's severed head had begun to decompose, the victors sent his scalp to the governor (Geiger 1937, 121). Finally, four years after Juanillo and his men killed Father Corpa, a Spanish report of 26 November 1601 advised that the last remnant of revolt had been put down (Geiger 1937, 121).

The Indian revolt had not discouraged Father Pareja's missionary efforts. In a letter to the king dated 8 March 1599, once he had praised the faith of the late Philip II and wished Philip III a long and happy tenure, Pareja broached the real issue, the Florida governor's mistreatment of the Indians. The governor required that they work without wages and that they furnish free food to the Spanish, he wrote (Geiger 1937, 129–31).

Pareja's letter was only the latest sally in a running battle between the government and the missionaries. Combined with Florida's bleak economic picture, the dissension led Philip III to consider abandoning the San Agustín fort and removing the Christian Indians to the Caribbean (Geiger 1937, 141). He also asked, in November 1600, for recommendations on Florida's future. Among those invited to contribute to the report was Father Pareja, who was identified as the vicar of San Juan del Puerto on the San Mateo (Geiger 1937, 143). Under his care were five hundred Christians in the villages Carabay (one-quarter league distant from San Juan), Vera Cruz (one-half league distant), Hicacharico (one league), Chinisca and San Pablo (one and a half leagues), San Mateo (two leagues), Arratoba (two and a half leagues), Potaya (four leagues), and

Nojo (five leagues).[4] Pareja, who spoke the Indian language, visited each village church to say mass and to attend to his parishioners' welfare.

In his declaration for the report, Pareja suggested that the governor needed to show more "enthusiasm and encouragement" for mission work and that he be commanded to deal impartially with Indians who disturbed the peace, whether Christian or not. The governor held the view that once an Indian became a Christian he was no longer to be punished. The chiefs who used to carry out tribal punishments, he observed, now "do not dare carry out these laws for fear of the governor, who does not want the Indians punished even though the offenses are public and notorious." Pareja favored moving the presidio north, where there was "land and not sandplots and marshlands like this place of St. Augustine," and where the population was greater and the harbors better for visiting ships. All the missionaries who contributed to the report agreed that the governor had failed to give them the aid and cooperation guaranteed by royal decrees (Geiger 1937, 129, 143, 146).

On 19 November 1602, as a result of the many complaints against him by the priests and others, the Council of the Indies decided to recall Governor Canzo. Before his recall, however, in January 1603, the governor toured Guale in a show of support for the priests who had resettled their missions following the Indian revolt. At San Pedro on Cumberland Island he helped Father López dedicate a church even more impressive than that at San Agustín, and on his way back to the presidio he stopped by San Juan where on 12 March he settled a dispute between the Indian queen Doña María and several of her chieftains (Geiger 1937, 163).

Florida's new governor, Pedro de Ybarra, landed at San Agustín on 19 October 1603. He had been captured en route from Spain by English pirates, escaped in a launch, was recaptured by the same pirates, who left him on the wild coasts of Cuba, and finally escaped to Havana for safe transit to Florida (Geiger 1937, 164, 165). Of the Christian Indian chiefs who paid him an early visit in Florida, he wrote that "they live as

4. A league is about three miles.

Trail on Fort George Island near the site of Pareja's mission. From Benjamin 1878.

Catholics and give very clear signs of the fruit the mission stations are producing in them." He urged Philip III to send twelve more friars to augment the five who remained (Geiger 1937, 167). The following year, Ybarra toured the missions, stopping first at Pareja's San Juan del Puerto where he assured the Indians that "his Majesty did not wish to take their lands nor any other thing, but desired that they become Christians, save their souls and on dying enter into heaven" (Geiger 1937, 172). The next year, 1605, brought the additional missionaries Ybarra had requested. The friars' workload was readjusted, with Father Pareja retaining San Juan (Geiger 1937, 186).

Only a year later, however, Governor Ybarra advised Philip III that his successor in Florida should be not only "a soldier known for his valor and ability" but "more than this . . . a holy man so that he will not be ruined by the friars, who will offer him plenty of occasions to test his virtue" (Geiger 1937, 221). To lessen the friction between the governor and the religious, the king sent the bishop of Cuba, Bishop Altamirano, who arrived in San Agustín on 15 March 1606, the first bishop to visit Florida since Bishop Suárez's trip with Pánfilo de Narváez in 1528 (Geiger 1937, 189). While in San Agustín, the bishop celebrated Easter Mass and confirmed 350 persons (Geiger 1937, 196).[5] He then set out to tour the missions, beginning with San Pedro, where among those he confirmed was Juan Quebedo, a chief at San Juan. After swinging north and west through the district, he returned to San Pedro and then spent 8–10 May with Father Pareja at San Juan, confirming 482 persons, including Doña María, the Indian queen. He returned to San Agustín on 12 May, then toured the missions to the south and west.

In Bishop Altamirano's report to Philip III he praised the governor and the friars and suggested that the chief cause of the friction between them lay in the friars' belief that "the Pope had given them the right of investiture with these Indian missions and provinces so that, to their way of thinking, they are Governors and Bishops of their parishes; and no one except their religious superiors can interfere with their jurisdiction, for they call it absolute" (Geiger 1937, 202). Governor Ybarra, on the other hand, argued that he held all temporal power in Spanish Florida (Geiger 1937, 192). Altamirano petitioned the king to define clearly the limits of power of the con-

5. These ceremonies marked the first administration of confirmation and holy orders in what is now the United States.

flicting parties (Geiger 1937, 202). His report eventually led to the reassignment out of Florida of the few priests identified as causing some of the conflict (Geiger 1937, 206). Father Pareja remained at San Juan.

The following year, 1607, Philip III recommended to Governor Ybarra that he reduce by half the military in Florida and consider removing Christian Indians for their protection to Española in the Caribbean. Ybarra sought the advice of the friars, which led Fathers Pareja and Piñaranda to write a letter of protest to the king on 20 November. If the military were weakened, they warned, the pagan Indians would destroy the Christian settlements. On the contrary, they begged the king, "protect the presidio and permit it to be strengthened." It would be a mistake to abandon the Florida missions where they were succeeding so well, and in fact "more religious should be sent to answer the needs of this field" (Geiger 1937, 211, 212). At the urgings of both the governor and the friars to support at least the status quo, Philip relented.

Relations between Ybarra and the friars remained strained, however, and Father Pareja continued to fight for church prerogatives and against any move he judged harmful to mission work. On 7 July 1608, the governor wrote the San Agustín friary asking Father Pareja, who was visiting there, to explain why two friars had boarded a vessel in San Agustín without governmental permission. Pareja replied that the visit to the ship was not without precedent, and, further, that the friars were on the bishop's business, not the Inquisition's, as Ybarra had assumed. Ybarra replied the same day that, while a bishop himself might pay such a visit, the friars' authority to do so was doubtful (Geiger 1937, 214). Pareja and Ybarra locked horns again over a government accountant named Mercado, a friend of the friars whom Ybarra viewed as a talkative troublemaker. Fearing that Mercado might be fired, Pareja set in motion an investigation in his defense, then wrote Ybarra that dismissing him would inconvenience the friars, for "in every need that we have experienced he has always assisted us and continues to visit us, our friars and churches" (Geiger 1937, 217). On a different front, Pareja objected that some of Ybarra's regulations impeded missionary visits to Indian settlements in the interior, and in yet another controversy he argued the merits of accepting and instructing novices in Florida rather than obtaining priests from Spain, an argument he lost in a Council of the Indies decision (Geiger, 1937, 220).

Still, by 1609, peace had been so far restored with the governor that Fathers Pareja and Serrono wrote the king on 5 May, "Praised be God that these difficulties have ceased by the use of proper remedies. . . . We live in great peace with your governor, Pedro de Ybarra who rules these provinces. . . . He has provided us with the things we have requested especially when they pertain to the spread of the faith, the augmentation of [Christian] Indians or of new *doctrinas*. In those which we have recently taken over he has given us what is necessary, showing at the same time his favor, which is not of the least importance" (Geiger 1937, 220). Pedro de Ybarra ended his term as governor on 20 October 1609.

By the end of the decade, Florida had become a custody of the Catholic church, with Father Pareja, still head of the San Juan mission, listed in 1610 as the custody's superior (Geiger 1937, 234). In 1612, the church designated the mainland a missionary province, Santa Elena, still answerable to provincial headquarters in Cuba. Santa Elena's first provincial was Father Juan Batista de Capella.

In July 1612, twenty friars arrived from Spain in answer to an urgent request by Florida's new governor, Juan Fernández de Olivera, who considered Florida primarily a mission field protected by a single fort. His attention to the missionaries' needs gained their enthusiastic support and added to the renewed hope they were feeling for their work. "We hold it for certain that the hour of God has arrived wherein all desire to become good Christians," the friars advised Philip III. "From very distant places the Indians come to seek baptism and to render obedience to your Majesty; a thing which is astounding to us religious who have been here from eighteen to twenty years civilizing and training Indians with so little hope of seeing this prosperous day" (Geiger 1937, 242). The religious community greatly regretted Governor Olivera's death later in 1612.

By this time, religious ceremonies at San Juan del Puerto were fairly elaborate. Indians traveled long distances to participate in mass and other functions on the principal feast days. They sang High Mass and vespers and during Holy Week carried in processional through the village beautifully crafted images of Christ and Mary. The impressive mission church, crowned with a bell tower complete with bells, was of heavy, rough-hewn timbers, with inside hewn planking and wattle and daub walls (Geiger 1937, 143; Milanich and Sturtevant 1972, 10).[6]

On 12 June 1614, Father Luis Gerónimo de Oré, a distinguished Peruvian scholar, received orders to report on Florida's missionary work. His lengthy account told of Father Pareja, that "good religious," the oldest of the friars and "a man of great virtue" who, "in order that he might be useful not only to [the Indians] of his own mission and district, but to all in that province and language of Timucua in which he is skilled for he has worked among them for more than twenty years . . . has written and published several books called *La Doctrina Cristiana* and *Catecismo* and *Confessionario* and other devotional tracts. These are always in the hands of the Indians. With ease many Indian men and women have learned to read in less than two months, and they write letters to one another in their own language" (Oré 1936, 103).

Pareja's lengthy testimony to Oré told of Indians from miles away who traveled to the San Juan mission to spend the weekend so they could be on hand for the religious ceremonies on both Saturday and Sunday. He reported that the Indians' superstitions were disappearing and that the Indians were in many cases more spiritual than the Spanish soldiers and helped with baptisms and with administering the sacraments to the sick. He also urged rebuilding the fortress of Santa Elena and increasing missionary work in that area (Oré 1936, 104–8).[7]

Father Oré returned to Florida two years later, on 6 November 1616, to hold a chapter, a general assembly of the missionaries. It would be held, he decided, not in San Agustín but

6. San Juan is an archaeological site, and digging has uncovered the outline of buildings and numerous artifacts.

7. Port Royal, South Carolina.

Illustration from Francisco Pareja's *Confessionario* showing a woman confessing while being tugged at by the devil. Courtesy New York Historical Society.

at San Buenaventura de Guadalquini in Guale, where provisions for Indians were stored and thus available for the conclave. The chapter extended across several days of religious services, masses, sermons, and mission business, including the election of Father Pareja as provincial (Oré 1936, 130–31; Geiger 1937, 260–63).

In spite of such apparent progress by the missions, Governor Juan de Treviño Guillamás was proving far less friendly than his predecessor, Governor Olivera. Since taking office on 22 May 1613, he had complained in an undated letter that Florida had too many friars and too few soldiers (Geiger 1937, 249). Twenty-nine friars had sailed for Florida during 1612 and 1613; Guillamás said that instead of the forty-three currently in the missions, eight or ten would suffice. His figures were rebutted by Pareja and others, who wrote on 14 January 1617 that Florida had only thirty-five friars and needed fifty. Furthermore, they countered, the number of soldiers might safely be reduced, and no soldiers should be stationed at the missions unless requested by a friar because the soldiers set bad exam-

ples. Pareja and others cautioned the king against believing
everything he heard in favor of the governor; if he chose not
to view such information as false, "without fear of scruple,"
he might "at least look upon it as suspicious" because the governor wielded "more kingly powers than your Majesty does in
his own kingdom." In fact, the friars concluded, "we believe
it would be of very great service to Our Lord and your Majesty to subordinate the government officials to some vice-
royalty or *audiencia*, if . . . it is not possible to send here men
who are Christians. This remedy would be sufficient," but the
ideal solution would be to send "someone who would walk with
the friars" (Geiger 1937, 250).

Guillamás's replacement, Governor Juan de Salinas, arrived
in Florida on 2 August 1618, some eighteen months later, to
find thirty-eight Franciscan friars engaged in mission work.
The record indicates that he reached a good accommodation
with Pareja, whose religious authority as Florida's provincial
theoretically extended from the Florida Keys to the North
Pole. By this decade of the early seventeenth century, an en-
lightened policy of persuasion in religious matters had replaced the coercive efforts of earlier Spaniards. This change,
which reaped a better harvest of converts than had the practices of Menéndez or even the French Laudonnière, was primarily the work of Father Pareja. Probably around this time
his San Juan mission, the prestigious provincial residence near
the mouth of the San Mateo, gave its name to the river, which
became known as the Río San Juan.

In 1620, a new provincial for the Santa Elena province was
elected, Father Alonso Pesquero. The last document that in-
disputably places Pareja in Florida is a petition of 1 September
1621 to the king signed simply "padre," characteristically asking for more priests and more financial support for the missions. However, a certificate dated 22 May 1626 in the introduction to the 1627 edition of Pareja's Catechism implies that
he was still alive and in Florida at that time.[8] Although some

8. A scholarly essay on Pareja's writings and publications may be found in
Milanich and Sturtevant 1972 (15), which lists the following works: *Ca-
thecismo en Lengua Castellana y Timuquana*, (Mexico, 1612), a prepa-
ration for baptism; *Confessionario en Lengua Castellana y Timuquana*,
(Mexico, 1613), an instruction in confession; *Arte y Pronunciacion en Lengua
Timuquana* (Mexico, 1614), a grammar and pronunciation guide in the

authorities believe that Pareja died in 1628 in Mexico where his books were published, no documentation shows that he was ever reassigned from San Juan del Puerto. The probability is that after serving among the Timucuan Indians for more than a third of a century, Father Francisco Pareja died at his mission on the Río San Juan in 1628 (Milanich and Sturtevant 1972, 15).

Timucuan and Spanish languages; *Cathecismo y Examen para los que Comulgan,* (Mexico, 1627), a catechism and examination for communicants in Spanish and Timucuan.

FOUR

∞∞∞∞∞∞∞∞∞∞∞∞∞∞∞∞∞∞∞∞∞∞∞∞∞∞∞∞∞∞∞∞∞∞∞

Edmund Gray

EDMUND GRAY COULDN'T RESIST A FRON-
tier. Other people's boundaries—geographic, political, economic, legal—challenged him. A Quaker planter and one of
Georgia's most influential politicians in the 1750s, Gray came
to Florida only toward the end of his life, in the late 1760s.
Variously described as a strong-willed and pestilent fellow and
as a man of infinite art and finesse, he settled west of the island
where Father Pareja's mission had stood a century and a half
earlier. This was Gray's last frontier: Black Hammock Island,
nestled among the tidewater tributaries of the river referred
to in contemporary official documents as the St. Juan's.

As a young man in the early 1700s, Gray was a planter on
the southwestern frontier of Virginia, where he adopted the
Quaker faith of some of his neighbors. The Society of Friends
by the 1650s often found itself at the center of political and
religious controversy all along America's northeastern seaboard, a circumstance that must have recommended the faith
to Gray. Even though he violated the Quaker prohibitions
against slaveholding and soldiering, Gray evidently recognized kindred thinking in the Friends' approach to matters of
religious and civil liberty.

Whereas Quakers in Massachusetts had been executed for
their preachings as recently as 1661, the young colony of Geor-

gia welcomed all persecuted Protestants, particularly Quakers.[1] Georgia's 1732 charter, which provided for liberty of conscience, also honored the Quaker interdiction against taking oaths by allowing Quakers in legal proceedings to substitute solemn affirmations for the oaths required of others (Hitz 1957, 10). Another comparatively liberal early Georgia law, however, discouraged most prosperous planters from settling there: Georgia prohibited all persons not at least part Indian from owning slaves (Wright 1981, 203; Abbot 1959, 21).[2] In 1750, to bring in needed settlers, Georgia opened her doors to all slaveholders, regardless of race.

On 27 February 1750 in Savannah, the main topic of discussion for the Council of Georgia was the admission of Edmund Gray as a settler. The council decided to approve a generous grant of land to Gray but to withhold similar grants to some of his Quaker followers whose reliability remained in some doubt. Gray brought his Quakers along anyway, parceling out land to them on his own authority in the first of many acts that would pit him against the established government wherever he settled. In this case, the council left him alone (Hawes 1951, 323). Gray's plantation, Brandon, and those of the other Friends were carved out of the colony's wildest and northernmost frontier. Near the headwaters of the Savannah River where it is joined by Little River (about twenty miles northwest of Augusta), this first Quaker settlement in Georgia was upriver from the tiny fort of Augusta and more than a hundred miles by water from the coastal capital, Savannah.

Gray did not yet enjoy the friendly relations he would later build with Indians farther south, and on 15 May 1751 he com-

1. Georgia was chartered in 1732 by England's King George II to a corporation, the Trustees for Establishing the Colony of Georgia in America, as a barrier colony to buffer the twelve British colonies to the north against incursion by the Spanish in Florida and the French in Louisiana. Among the original trustees was James Oglethorpe, who in the 1740s led two unsuccessful British attacks on St. Augustine. The colony guaranteed religious liberty to all except Catholics.

2. Including Indians would have made the law unenforceable. Before the colonization of America, Indians often made slaves of their prisoners of war, a practice Europeans adopted in the early days of colonization. Under the pretense that the Indians were prisoners, Europeans frequently enslaved those who refused to accept Christianity.

plained to John Fallowfield, a friend in South Carolina, about a "half- Breed Fellow" from the Cherokee Nation who had persuaded six of his black slaves to join the Cherokees, "from whence he promised to conduct them to some Place where they might depend on their Freedom." Although three of the slaves chose to return, Gray warned his friend that because the Cherokee "is a subtil Fellow, he may have the like Influence on many slaves in South Carolina. It's necessary some Expedient should be fallen on to prevent a practice of such dangerous Consequences. He ought to be proceeded against, as an Incendiary and Disturber of the publick Safety" (McDowell 1958–70, 1:83).

In 1752 the Georgia trustees gave up their twenty-year-old charter, and in 1754 George II reorganized the colony as a royal province and appointed John Reynolds its first royal governor (Abbot 1959, 3–56). In only a few months, Governor Reynolds managed to alienate most of the colonists with his inattention to duty and his overreliance on his incompetent and corrupt assistant, William Little. Edmund Gray, by now the most powerful political figure in the colony after Reynolds, openly despised the governor. Gray set out to ensure his own election and the election of a slate of others to Georgia's first elected legislature, to meet in 1755. With Reynolds's failures his primary target, Gray spoke convincingly to the colonists' love of liberty and desire for economic success (Abbot 1959, 38–43, 46–53; Hamer 1929, 1–2).

Gray was elected. In order to attract more settlers, he immediately urged his fellow legislators to reduce the landholding prerequisite for voting and to relax the cultivation requirements for new landholders. When Reynolds objected, Gray and other legislators he had helped elect appealed to King George. Gray also petitioned to seat some men he had supported for the legislature whom he felt had been improperly declared not elected. When the Georgia House of Assembly rejected his petition, Gray and six other members stayed away from the sessions, hoping to preclude a quorum for the conduct of legislative business. The dissidents expected the king to send support for Gray's petition, and in the meantime on 15 January 1755 they circulated a letter summoning to Savannah all who "regard the liberties of your country." Although Gray claimed he only wanted to seat the men who had been wrongly declared defeated, the letter so alarmed the governor that he organized a militia to defend the colony and had Gray and his fellow dissidents expelled from the legislature.

Gray fled south with scores of supporters and their families to settle "on those Lands between Altamaha and Saint Juan's Streams, a Country of one Degree in Latitude, esteemed neutral Lands, which were not to be settled either by the English or Spaniards," according to the field notes of William Gerard de Brahm, commissioned by the British to survey Georgia and Florida. Gray was now in a position to defy two governments. De Brahm's notes continue: "All persons incapable or unwilling to satisfy their Creditors, as also Men guilty of criminal Actions, would resort both from the English and Spaniards to said Edmond Grey, who, when ordered away by the Spaniards, he moved to the river Altamaha and when ordered away by the English, he did pretend to go and settle on the south side of St. Mary's [River]; thus deluding both English and Spaniards" (De Vorsey 1971, 148).

In fact, Gray created the settlement of New Hanover on the banks of the Satilla River, well south of the Altamaha, then Georgia's southern border. Stretching for miles in every direction, the thinly settled community centered on a fort that Gray built on the river.[3] South Carolina also claimed this land, maintaining a small garrison at its eastern edge on Cumberland Island. Like England, Spain claimed all the land south of the Altamaha, an area also claimed by the Lower and Upper Creeks and by Mary Musgrove Bosomworth, a half-breed who said that the other Indians had deeded their rights to her and her husband.

It was Mary Bosomworth from whom came his own title to New Hanover, Edmund Gray maintained, and matching wits with incensed counterclaimants must have afforded him a great deal of continuing enjoyment. Bosomworth, who proclaimed herself to be of royal Indian descent, with some right

3. After Gray left, Indians burned this fort—hence the site's modern name, Burnt Fort, Georgia, where today the White Oak–Kingland Road crosses the Satilla. See Marguerite Reddick Camden's *Challenge* (Jacksonville: Paramount Press, 1976), 195–98.

asserted title to more land in Georgia than any other individual. She had been interpreter, negotiator, and close personal friend to James Oglethorpe, one of Georgia's original trustees, and his main envoy to the Indians. From Oglethorpe and her Indian relatives, Bosomworth and three successive husbands had secured at least color of title to vast acreages from the Savannah to the St. Marys.[4]

Things had begun to heat up within a year of the settlers' arrival at New Hanover, according to a letter of 16 September 1756 from Governor Reynolds to South Carolina's Governor Lyttleton. "In the Beginning of last April," Gray's adversary wrote from Savannah, "one Edmund Gray, who is the Leader of that Gang, wrote to Mrs. Bosomworth who was then here, begging of her to come directly among them, and use her Interest with the Indians, in pacifying them, who had threatened to attack that Settlement, and she did for that Time make Things easy between them." The temporary truce gave the governor small comfort, however. Underestimating his opponents was apparently not one of Reynolds's shortcomings: "As they are a lawless Crew, consisting of about 50 or 60 Gunmen, they may very probably involve us in some future Broils with the Indians, unless they are removed, or put under some Regulation" (McDowell 1958–70, 2:194).

Meanwhile, New Hanover settlers petitioned George II for recognition and on 3 February 1756 drew up a compact to govern themselves until the king either set them up as an independent entity or placed them under the government of South Carolina or Georgia. The compact regulated such matters as allotment of lands, taxes, erecting and maintaining a fort, and cattle sales. A provision to preserve trees "for the encouragement of New Settlers" forbade anyone to "cut any Cedar, Cypress, white or Red Oak Timber on Vacant Lands within fifteen miles of town." Commissioners were to meet on the first Tuesday of the month (Hamer 1929, 4, Appendix A, 52).

On 16 February 1757, Samuel Lloyd of Georgia wrote William Russell in London about another action by the Gray-Bosomworth alliance, this time evidently against a fellow colo-

4. For biographical details on Mary Bosomworth see Coulter 1927 and Corry 1941.

nist. "I dout not of your zealous endeavors, by Your Self and friends, to procure justice be done to poor Mr. Robinson about his lands which the intrigues of Bosomworth and Gray are endeavoring to wrest from him" (Bevan n.d., 61).

By this time, Gray and New Hanover had alienated nearly every authority involved with the settlement. South Carolina's Governor Lyttleton had somewhat contradictory fears: that the Spanish king might go to war over New Hanover's presence on Spanish-claimed territory and that the New Hanover settlers, who traded in St. Augustine, might become spies for the Spanish (Gold 1969, 128; Bolton 1925, 103–4). The Spanish governor of Florida had in fact offered Gray protection if he would settle on the St. Johns in Indian trade. He rejected this offer, and thirty-four armed men were sent from St. Augustine to order Gray back across the Altamaha, frightening him into moving for a short time to Cumberland Island.

The settlement's only supporter appeared to be Georgia's new governor, Henry Ellis, who had replaced Reynolds in February 1757. On 5 May, Ellis wrote George II's London agent for colonial affairs, the Board of Trade, that while traveling on the southern frontier of Georgia he "accidently saw that odd character Gray, who occasioned so much disturbance here at Mr. Reynold's arrival." Gray, he wrote, had "entered into a connection with" a man named Alexander, a longtime friend of the Lower Creeks and influential among them, who had "prevailed upon some of the chiefs of these people to go to Augustine and threaten the Spaniards with a War, if for the future they presume to molest or disturb" the New Hanover settlers. In retaliation, "and alarmed by some of the indian irregularitys," the Spanish governor offered Gray and Alexander his protection if they would "settle upon the River St. Johns, & establish an indian trade." Although Gray told Governor Ellis this offer would support British claims to the lands north of the St. Johns if only Ellis would license Gray to trade there, the governor judged this a "dangerous experiment, as it would afford an opportunity to the Spaniards of practicing on these Savages" and possibly seducing them to change sides. Indian loyalties weren't the only ones Ellis distrusted, for he added that he feared "Gray might turn Traitor"; to dissuade him from settling on the St. Johns, he proposed instead that

Edmund Gray's Sawpit Bluff in the 1770s. From Benjamin 1878.

Gray center his trade on "the River St. Mary's opposite to
Fort William." Gray agreed, Ellis wrote, "& he now seems inclined to quit the character of Legislator, which he has long
assumed for that of a Merchant.—he is a shrewd sensible fellow, affects an austerity of manners by which he has acquired
a considerable influence among the people of this Colony &
made some impression upon the Indians; & if he can be managed may prove an useful instrument in many respects." Fi-

nally, Ellis suggested that since Gray and his men often went to St. Augustine they could gather intelligence information for the British, serving as "a kind of advanced party not to say Barrier, against the Spaniards & their Indian allies of Florida."[5]

The Board of Trade rejected the New Hanover petition on 21 April 1758. Being unimpressed with Governor Ellis's reasoning about granting Gray a license to trade with Indians on the St. Marys, it wrote the governor that this "counteracts every other prudent step you appear to have taken to remove the jealousies and suspicions [the Spanish Florida governor] had entertained of your having secretly encouraged and supported the hostilities which the Creek Indians had committed in the settlements under his protection: for whatever other motives the Indians may have had for attacking the Spaniards, there is great ground to suspect that Gray may have had his views in instigating them to it." The board ordered Ellis and Lyttleton to send commissioners to tell Gray to break up the settlement (*American State Papers*, 51).

In January 1759, the commissioners "rowed up to the settlement" of New Hanover, according to the report of South Carolina commissioner Major Hyrne. There they met with several of the inhabitants, including "Mr. Edmund Gray, the person of chief influence and greatest sway among them. He entered very freely into conversation with us on the subject of our Errand" and claimed himself more than ready to obey the king's orders. He also pointed out one small snag. The men who owned the most property were so in debt that they could return neither to South Carolina nor to Georgia and might, he feared, "be induced to go over to the Spaniards, from whom he knew they had received strong invitations and Promises of Encouragement." Commissioner Hyrne in turn suggested "how dangerous such a step would be" for these Englishmen, living under a different system of government among people of a different religion, who "would always watch them with a jealous eye and be ready to take all advantages against them" (Hamer 1929, 10).

5. Henry Ellis to Board of Trade, Savannah, 5 May 1757, *Colonial Records of Georgia*, vol. 28, pt. 1-A, 18ff.

The deadline set for breaking up the settlement was 1 March, two months after the commissioners' visit. Gray promised to try to get his followers to abandon New Hanover and to use force to oust them, if necessary. On the deadline date, the settlers orchestrated the appearance of moving out, but only a few of them actually complied with the orders. Edmund Gray remained.

The following year, Governor Ellis, aware that Gray had never abandoned New Hanover and his regular southern haunts, assigned him to stir up the Lower Creeks against the Cherokees who had been molesting settlers in western Georgia and South Carolina. Many tribes served as pawns in the Seven Years' War between France and England, the Cherokees in this instance spurred on by the French in settlements west of British America. On 14 April 1760, a council meeting document reported that a triumphant party of Creeks "who had been fitted out for War against the Cherokees at the Expence of this Government, this Day arrived at Savannah with three Cherokee Scalps (conducted by Edmund Gray who had gone with them through the Settlements). They Entred the Town, the Enemies Scalps being born before them, singing their War Songs; and were saluted by a Discharge of the Cannon." The Indians, presumably accompanied by Gray, "marched through in Triumph to the Council Chamber," where a grateful Governor Ellis congratulated them on their success (*Colonial Records of Georgia* 1907, 8:284; Bolton 1925, 106).

Governor Ellis resigned in November and was succeeded by James Wright.[6] Less than a year later, on 15 September 1761, Georgia's council recommended that Wright approve Edmund Gray's application for a renewal of his license to trade with the Indians on Cumberland Island (*Colonial Records of Georgia* 1907, 8:569). Although he granted the license (Bolton 1925, 106), the governor was concerned about settlers occupying land in the supposedly neutral zone and reported them to

6. Governor Ellis had suffered greatly in the Georgia climate. Walking Savannah's sandy streets, he had carried an umbrella for shade and customarily dangled "a thermometer from it at the height of his nostrils" so he could appreciate just how hot it was. Even his weekend home twelve miles out of town, he complained, offered little relief (Abbot 1959, 57, 82).

the Board of Trade on 17 October. First, there were the New Hanover settlers, who flouted the king's command to move in 1759: "These people, in the whole, amount to between seventy and eighty men, and are a mixture of renagates from the two Carolinas, Virginia, etc. etc. . . . scattered about the country and on lands at present not in my jurisdiction or authority." Furthermore, even though the nominal boundary of Georgia was the Altamaha, Wright wrote, "General Oglethorpe extended his settlements southward without any regard to that boundary and many plantations were settled far beyond the Altamaha, and marks of possession held and the lands claimed to St. Juan's River." Adding to Governor Wright's agitation was Fort William on the southern end of Cumberland Island, occupied by a guard unit from South Carolina "not under my direction or authority, but of the Governor of South Carolina" (Gold 1969, 128).

Just two months later, Spain's entry on 16 December 1761 into the Seven Years' War on the side of the French made Governor Wright's worries moot, and Edmund Gray's presence in the formerly neutral lands in fact worked to Georgia's benefit. The following year Spain suffered her worst defeat of the war when the British occupied Havana. In 1763, the peace treaty returned Cuba to Spain but took Florida from her. Florida went to England, and France awarded Louisiana to Spain in compensation.

In the aftermath of the war, England's George III, who had taken the throne in 1760, issued a proclamation on 7 October 1763 that settled the dispute over the Georgia-Florida border once and for all.[7] The proclamation adopted the recommendation of Florida's new governor, Grant, to extend Florida north to the St. Marys River on the grounds that the St. Johns River valley would attract settlers to the new colony. The Georgia line was pushed south to the St. Marys to eliminate the claims of South Carolina. The proclamation also reflected the king's intent to improve treatment of the Indians. It protected them against loss of their lands to unscrupulous frontiersmen and

---

7. This document is printed in full in the *South Carolina Gazette*, 21 December 1763 (copy in the Bennett Collection).

against unlicensed traders. Henceforth, the Indians would be wards of the crown.

Edmund Gray once again answered the call of a new frontier. He built his plantation and Indian trading post on Black Hammock Island, west of Fort George Island near the mouth of the St. Johns River. In the yard he built a sawmill and a

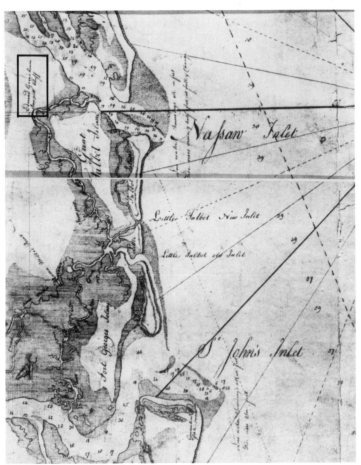

Map showing location of Edmund Gray's plantation on Black Hammock Island. From map 53 of William Gerard de Brahm's maps in the Library of Congress, Map Division (original in the British Museum).

rectangular sawpit for shaping lumber. The official surveyor's "Inhabitants of East Florida, 1763 to 1771" and their "Employs, Business and Qualifications in Science" listed "Edmond Gray, planter" still living on Black Hammock Island in 1771 (De Vorsey 1971, 182). On one map of the tidewater area, the surveyor, De Brahm, recorded the exact location of Gray's house.[8] (The 1777 Patriot attack on Florida during the American Revolution would rendezvous here.)

The names Sawpit Bluff, where Edmund Gray's plantation house stood, and Sawpit Creek, the waterway that flowed in front of the house, persist to this day. The outlines of Gray's sawpit, though overgrown with trees and heavy brush, can still be traced. So can the fallen walls of his tabby house near the shoreline of the bluff, perhaps the oldest remains of a European dwelling in the St. Johns River valley.[9] Such staying power, strength, and persistence in the face of adversity serve as a fitting monument to a man who regarded every frontier as a personal challenge.

8. See illustrations in De Vorsey (1971) and Map 53 in the De Brahm Collection, Map Division, Library of Congress.

9. Tabby is a building material made of oyster shells, lime, and sand, mixed with salt water.

FIVE

William Bartram

IN 1765, ABOUT THE TIME EDMUND GRAY'S tabby house was going up on Black Hammock Island and two hundred years after Nicolas Barré and Jean Ribault charted the northeast Florida coast, young William Bartram was exploring the St. Johns River with his botanist father, John. On 7 June, John Bartram wrote that King George had appointed him the king's chief botanist and ordered him to "go directly to Florida" to study that subtropical peninsula that England had acquired from Spain two years earlier. Would William care to go along as his assistant? "As thee wrote to me last winter and seemed so very desirous to go there," the Quaker father wrote his son, "now thee hath a fair opportunity; so pray let me know as soon as possible" (Darlington [1849] 1967, 424).

The elder Bartram, self-taught in botany and other sciences, had begun farming in 1728 at Kingsessing, near Philadelphia. There he also established the botanical gardens that would bring him fame, and there William had been born on 9 February 1739 (Fagin 1933, 1). William Bartram in his teens had about four years of formal education, then explored with his father various wild regions of North America, including the Catskill Mountains (Earnest 1940, 54). He was twenty-six when he left a rather unsuccessful mercantile venture at

Cape Fear, North Carolina, to join his father's expedition to Florida.

Traveling through South Carolina and into Georgia, on 1 October at Fort Bennington the two men identified the first of many new plants they would discover on their travels, a species of flowering bush they named Franklinia in honor of a family friend, Benjamin Franklin. (Franklin had earlier offered William a job in his Philadelphia printing shop [Darlington (1849) 1967, 207].)

On 8 October, the Bartrams crossed the St. Marys River by swimming their horses across into Florida at what is now King's Ferry. Among their first observation sites was Cabbage Swamp, where displays of cabbage or sabal palms stand untouched still. It was about four miles south of where the colonial path from Savannah to St. Augustine crossed the Little St. Marys River. "Hereabout," John Bartram noted in his diary for 9 October, "we observed ye tree palm growed 30 feet high & held thro several bay swamps." By the next evening they had crossed at Cowford on the St. Johns River and "lodged under a pine" in the thinly settled area where Jacksonville lies today (Bartram 1942, 33).

Now the Bartrams' most intense study would begin, for they had reached the primary site of their explorations, the St. Johns River valley, which they would investigate to its distant southerly origins. By 27 December they had visited a number of major springs that fed the river, including Salt Springs, and on 28 December they explored Mount Royal, an impressive Indian mound on the river's west bank.[1] In his diary, along with detailed descriptions of plants and animals observed, John Bartram included terse comments on the day's events, the terrain, and the weather. On 9 February, for example, on their return trip, he described a marsh below Cowford "on both sides then pines, then another pretty large marsh and so on alternately high oak banks, open marshes and flat pine woods and savannahs; back there is pretty high sand hills and some ponds." Proceeding seaward, he assessed the strategic value of St. John's Bluff and discussed "a large rich

1. Salt Springs lies west of Lake George in the Ocala National Forest, Mount Royal on the north side of Fruitland Cove.

island," Fort George, where "Hazard . . . a good kind of man, and one of the best planters in Florida" lived. "[We] walked all over the island," Bartram wrote, "observing his improvements; and the curiosities both natural and artificial, of the Indians and Spaniards"—the Indian mounds, for instance, and the cedar posts and pieces of hewn live oaks that showed "the Spaniards had a fine settlement here" (Bartram 1942, 47, 48).[2]

John Bartram went home to Philadelphia but "left my son Billy in Florida," he wrote his old friend and patron in England, Peter Collinson, in June 1766. "Nothing will do with him now but he will be a planter upon St. Johns River, about twenty four miles from Augustine, and six from the Fort of Picolata. This frolic of his, and our maintenance, hath drove me to great straits" (Darlington [1849] 1967, 281).

Although William Bartram's consuming interests lay in scientific discovery and in recording his discoveries in writing and drawings, he meant to make a success of his modest rice and indigo plantation with the six slaves his father had given him.[3] Henry Laurens wrote John Bartram on 9 August after visiting William that the farm, on the east bank of the St. Johns, was "the least agreeable of all the places" he had seen. Having never run a farm before, William had built "on a low sheet of sandy pine barren, verging on the swamp," Laurens wrote, "which before his door is very narrow, in a bight or cove of the river so shoal and covered with umbrellas that the common current is lost and the water almost stagnated" (Darlington [1849] 1967, 439).

William himself was little better off, according to Laurens, who would one day preside over the Continental Congress: "The swamp and adjoining marsh . . . will require more strength to put them in tolerable order than Mr. Bartram is at present possessed of to make any progress above daily bread, and that of a coarse kind, too. . . . His own health very imperfect. He had the fever when I was first with him and

2. "Hazard" may have been Richard Hazzard, who settled New Hanover with Edmund Gray; see Hamer 1929, 55.

3. For a discussion of the plantation's precise location, see John Bartram (1942, 69, 76): "about the mouth of Six Mile Creek" and "a point where the road from Picolata ends on the south shore of the cove at the mouth of Six Mile Creek."

looked very poorly the second visit. . . . No colouring can do justice to the forlorn state of poor Billy Bartram" (Darlington [1849] 1967, 438).

On 26 August, John Bartram again wrote Collinson in despair over William: "I am afraid all will be thrown away upon him. He is so whimsical and so unhappy as not to take any of his friends advice. Mr. DeBr[ahm] wanted him to go with him to draw draughts for him, in his survey of Florida; but Billy would not, though by that journey he would have had the finest opportunity of seeing the country and its productions" (Darlington [1849] 1967, 283).[4]

Early in 1767, William Bartram abandoned his Florida farm and returned to Pennsylvania, supporting himself there for a time as a day laborer, then moving again to Cape Fear, North Carolina. The solution to all his problems, Peter Collinson suggested, was marriage. "If my advice may have any weight with him," Collinson wrote John Bartram on 10 April 1767, "it is to get him a good, notable wife,—a farmer's daughter, and return to his estate and set his shoulders heartily to work to improve it" (Darlington [1849] 1967, 287). Because Collinson appreciated William's beautiful drawings, having bought them from him as well as many newly discovered plants and seeds, he hoped a wife would inspire William to earn a substantial, steady income that would support his scientific and artistic avocations. But William Bartram was in love with nature.

Collinson died the following year, with William no closer to marriage and as enthusiastic as ever about further exploration of the St. Johns River valley. The Bartrams' new patron was Dr. John Fothergill, an English physician friend and fellow Quaker.[5] In 1772, Fothergill agreed to underwrite the costs of William's proposed explorations in Florida and other southern areas (Darlington [1849] 1967, 345).

William Bartram sailed from Philadelphia for Charleston on 20 March 1773 (Bartram 1943, 172)[6] on the first leg of a four-

4. The British government commissioned De Brahm to survey the southern British colonies. See De Vorsey (1971).

5. For John Fothergill's biographical details, see Darlington ([1849] 1967, 333).

6. In *Travels of William Bartram* ([1791] 1940), Bartram often confused dates, as in this case: In *Travels*, he gave this date as April 1773. See Bartram 1943, 172; see also 145, 180–82.

William Bartram, portrait by Charles Willson Peale. Courtesy Independence
National Historical Park, Philadelphia.

year journey that would take him not only through the St.
Johns River valley but, as revolutionary war fever rose,
through the Carolinas, Georgia, and Alabama to the Gulf of
Mexico and the Mississippi. After only a few weeks, Bartram
left Charleston for Savannah, which would become his base of
explorations for nearly a year of scientific forays along the
Georgia coast and into the Indian backlands. In early May
1773, Bartram hired an assistant, seventeen-year-old John

McIntosh. Later that month, at an Indian congress at Augusta, the two men heard about an outbreak of Indian uprisings in Florida. Bartram also contracted a severe fever during this time, and his illness, combined with the news of the Florida Indians, caused him to postpone crossing the Florida border.

Not until the spring of 1774, probably in April, did Bartram and McIntosh arrive at the southern tip of Cumberland Island, where the pilot of the *St. Mary's* took them across to Amelia Island in Florida. The supervisor of Lord Egmont's plantation on the island's northern end, Mr. Egan, entertained them for several days, then went south with them, his slaves rowing their boat down the inland passage toward the St. Johns. The party spent a night in the open on the northern tip of Talbot Island, where they roasted oysters and fought off mosquitoes with a spectacular campfire (Bartram 1943, 145).

Traveling upstream from the island at the mouth of the St. Johns, the men dined at the indigo plantation of Francis Philip Fatio, Sr., on the south bank just east of Newcastle Creek.[7] Bartram was especially interested in Fatio's garden, which boasted "a greater variety than any other in the coliny," including "a variety of European grapes imported from the Streight, olives, figs, pomgranates, filberts, oranges, lemons, a variety of garden flowers from Europe, itc." From Fatio's, the party "continued up the river 5 or 10 miles, got to Pottburg, a large plantation belonging to a gentleman in England. Here we stayed this night & in the morning Mr. Egan set off by land to Augustine, having business with the Governor" (Bartram 1943, 145).

McIntosh elected to stay behind at Cowford after the overnight stay at nearby Pottburg, which Bartram "did not greatly regret. . . . Each of our pursuits were perhaps equally laudable; and upon this supposition, I was quite willing to part with

---

7. For a brief biography of the Swiss Fatio, see Gold (1929, 54). A family history and greater detail may be found in Susan L'Engle (1888, 2–10) and Gertrude L'Engle (1951, 1:14–40; 1949 vol. 2). A plat of the St. Johns Fatio plantation is on file at Florida Private Claims 2:282, Record Group 49, National Archives. In 1794, John McIntosh bought the plantation directly to the east. Tabby foundations believed to be of the Fatio plantation still exist in 1989.

William Bartram's drawing of the Florida Sandhill Crane. Courtesy British
Museum of Natural History.

him upon amicable terms." Their views, Bartram wrote,
"were probably totally opposite; [McIntosh was] a young me-
chanic on his adventures" looking for a busy port where he
could make a comfortable living or even a fortune, "whilst I,
continually impelled by a restless spirit of curiosity, in pursuit
of new productions of nature, my chief happiness consisted in

tracing and admiring the infinite power, majesty and perfection of the great Almighty Creator, and in the contemplation, that through divine aid and permission, I might be instrumental in discovery and introducing into my native country, some original production of nature, which might become useful to society" ([1791] 1940, 82).

At Pottburg, Bartram wrote, "the inhabitants [were] greatly alarmed at the hostile disposition of the Indians & were generally on the flight or fortifying themselves by stockadeing in their houses. . . . I purchased a canoe and alone continued my voyage up the river, having a sail, some provisions, gun and ammunition. My undertaking was I confess somewhat hazardous at such a time" (Bartram 1943, 145).

Not far upstream, Bartram went ashore on the west bank, "being struck with the magnificence of a venerable grove of Live Oak, Palms and Laurel [*magnolia grandiflora*]." In one of his less detailed botanical notes, he would later describe the magnolia as "silvered with white flowers. . . . Their usual height is about one hundred feet, and some greatly exceed that. The trunk is perfectly erect, rising in the form of a beautiful column supporting a head like an obtuse cone. The flowers are on the extremities of the subdivisions of the branches in the center of a coronet of dark green . . . perfectly white, and expanded like a full blown rose" (Bartram [1791] 1940, 83, 91).

A more typical entry about cypress trees reflects Bartram's care for explicit detail and his poetic approach to nature, a flowery contrast to his father's terse descriptions. His romantic style would influence the works of a number of contemporary and later literary figures, among them Coleridge, Wordsworth, Shelley, Tennyson, Carlyle, Emerson, and Thoreau (Fagin 1933, 127–98).

The Cupressus disticha stands in the first order of North American trees. Its majestic stature is surprising; and on approaching it, we are struck with a kind of awe, at beholding the stateliness of the trunk, lifting its cumbrous top towards the skies, and casting a wide shade upon the ground, as a dark intervening cloud, which, for a time, excludes the rays of the sun. The delicacy of its colour, and texture of its leaves, exceed every thing in vegetation. It generally grows in the water, or in low flat lands, near the banks of great rivers and lakes, that are covered, great part of the year, with two or three feet depth of water; and that part of the trunk which is subject to be under water, and four or five feet higher up, is greatly enlarged by prodigious buttresses, or pilasters, which in full grown trees, project out on every side, to such a distance, that several men might easily hide themselves in the hollows between. Each pilaster terminates under ground, in a very large, strong, serpentine root, which strikes off, and branches every way, just under the surface of the earth: and from these roots grow woody cones, called cypress knees, four, five, and six inches high, and from six to eighteen inches and two feet in diameter at their bases. The large ones are hollow, and serve very well for bee-hives; a small space of the tree itself is hollow, nearly as high as the buttresses already mentioned. From this place, the tree, as it were, takes another beginning, forming a grand straight column eighty or ninety feet high, when it divides every way around into an extensive flat horizontal top, like an umbrella, where eagles have their secure nests, and cranes and storks their temporary resting-places; and what adds to the magnificence of their appearance is the streamers of long moss that hang from the lofty limbs and float in the winds. This is their majestic appearance when standing alone, in large rice plantations, or thinly planted on the banks of great rivers.

Parroquets are commonly seen hovering and fluttering on their tops: they delight to shell the balls, its seed being their favourite food. The trunks of these trees, when hollowed out, make large and durable pettiaugers and canoes, and afford excellent shingles, boards, and other timber, adapted to every purpose in frame buildings. When the planters fell these mighty trees, they raise a stage round them, as high as to reach above the buttresses; on this stage, eight or ten negroes ascend with their axes, and fall to work round its trunk. I have seen trunks of these trees that would measure eight, ten, and twelve feet in diameter, and forty and fifty feet straight shaft. (Bartram [1791] 1940, 94– 95)

Bartram set down detailed descriptions not only of plants, birds, fish, trees, and insects but of places. He wrote of Mount Royal, for instance, where he and his father had gone ashore nearly ten years earlier. Bartram found himself moved by the grandeur of the great Indian mound, which lies near the St. Johns and in the vicinity of Drayton Island.

What greatly contributed towards completing the magnificence of the scene, was a noble Indian highway, which led from the great mount, on a straight line, three quarters of a mile, first through a point or wing of the orange grove, and continuing thence through an awful forest of live oaks, it was terminated by palms and laurel magnolias, on the verge of an oblong artificial lake, which was on the edge of an extensive green level savanna. This grand highway was about fifty yards wide, sunk a little below the common level, and the earth thrown up on each side, making a bank of about two feet high. Neither nature nor art could any where present a more striking contrast, as you approached this savanna. (Bartram [1791] 1940, 101–2)[8]

Traveling alone, Bartram survived many encounters with wild animals. Alligators several times tried to attack him, and he witnessed a fight between two of them. One rushed forward, Bartram wrote,

his plaited tail brandished high [as] his enormous body swells . . . when immediately from the opposite coast of the lagoon, emerges from the deep his rival champion. They suddenly dart upon each other. The boiling surface of the lake marks their rapid course, and a terrific conflict commences. They now sink to the bottom folded together in horrid wreaths. The water becomes thick and discoloured. Again they rise, their jaws clap together, re-echoing through the deep surrounding forests. Again they sink, when the contest ends at the muddy bottom of the lake, and the vanquished makes a hazardous escape, hiding himself in the muddy turbulent waters and sedge on a distant shore. The proud victor exulting returns to the place of action. The shores and forests resound his dreadful roar, to-

8. For an able discussion of Mount Royal as it probably once looked and as it looks today, see William H. Morgan, *Prehistoric Architecture in the Eastern United States* (Cambridge: MIT Press, 1980), 125–26.

William Bartram's drawing of the Florida Alligator. Courtesy British Museum of Natural History.

gether with the triumphing shouts of the plaited tribes around, witnesses of the horrid combat. (Bartram [1791] 1940, 115)

Despite such frightening scenes, Bartram managed a sort of universal love for nearly every animal, plant, or insect he observed, an affection that extended to the Indians at a time when they were viewed with apprehension by most non-Indians. He was called Puc Puggy, flower hunter, by the Seminoles (Bartram [1791] 1940, 162). In later years he would prepare an antislavery address, apparently meant for a congressional audience, in which he warned, "Consider God is no respector of Persons & that the Black, White, Red & Yellow People are equally dear to him, and under this protection and favour & that sooner or later ye must render full retribution" (McInnis 1979, 144).

After about a year in Florida, Bartram returned to Charleston. From there, he set out on the second half of his travels on 22 April 1775, three days after the battle of Lexington. He first visited the Indian lands in the Carolinas, then continued his botanical observations, traveling south through central Georgia and Alabama to the Gulf of Mexico and from there to the Mississippi River, where he reported that certain areas along the banks were suitable for substantial settlement.[9] In those early days of the Revolution, many Americans viewed the war more as a move to redress grievances than as a fight for independence. Many of Bartram's Quaker friends, including Benjamin Franklin, were busy trying to bring about a peaceful conclusion to colonial unrest. Still, as early as January 1776, at the request of Georgia's delegates, alarmed at their colony's proximity to the numerous British troops in East Florida, Congress recommended "the reduction of St. Augustine" (Bennett 1970, iii). The Declaration of Independence on 4 July crystallized most patriotic sentiment in favor of immediate independence. Even John Fothergill, Bartram's Quaker patron in England, advised American Friends not to oppose the independence movement (Harper 1953, 576).

In the turbulent months of late 1776, William Bartram reportedly volunteered for a detachment raised by his friend Lachlan McIntosh, uncle to John McIntosh, to repel an anticipated invasion of Georgia from St. Augustine by the British. He was offered a lieutenant's commission to remain in the army, but when the invasion proved to be a false rumor and McIntosh disbanded the detachment, Bartram resumed his travels (Harper 1953, 573).

By January 1777, Bartram was back with his father at Kingsessing, where he became partners with his brother John in managing the botanical gardens (Darlington [1849] 1967, xiv). It has been conjectured that an unsuccessful love affair with his cousin Mary Bartram in North Carolina may explain why William Bartram "never married, and why he buried himself for four years in the wilderness" (Earnest 1940, 98). Meanwhile, John had been deeded the gardens by their father in 1771 when William was at work in the Cape Fear area (Earnest 1940, 109; McInnis 1979, 13). John Bartram, Sr., died on 22 September, nine months after William's return.

William Bartram by now had built a reputation as a scholar

9. We now know that British authorities at the time considered moving the capital of West Florida from Pensacola to the Mississippi to take advantage of its navigational assets and to provide safe haven for local British loyalists (Harper 1953, 571–77; McInnis 1979, 180–95).

and traveler, although *The Travels of William Bartram* would not be published until 1791.[10] Visitors to the gardens included presidents and prominent scientists, congressmen, and writers. George Washington made two trips to the gardens at the time of the Constitutional Convention in Philadelphia in 1787. On 14 July of that year, a group arrived which included James Madison, George Mason, and Alexander Hamilton to find Bartram barefoot, hoeing in the garden (Fagin 1933, 25; Earnest 1940, 163). André Michaux, the French botanist, visited in 1789, 1792, and 1794. Thomas Jefferson, a longtime correspondent of Bartram's, lived for a time in the 1790s across the Schuylkill River from Kingsessing. Jefferson urged Bartram to take more exploratory trips, but failing eyesight and ill health kept him home.

Author and artist William Dunlap described a 1797 visit to Bartram, then fifty-eight.

May 9. Rise about 5 o'clock, and join Charles Brockden Brown about 6, for the purpose of walking to Bartram's Botanic Garden. . . . Arrived at the Botanist's Garden, we approached an old man who, with a rake in his hand, was breaking the clods of earth in a tulip bed. His hat was old and flapped over his face, his coarse shirt was seen near his neck, as he wore no cravat or kerchief; his waistcoat and breeches were both of leather, and his shoes were tied with leather strings. We approached and accosted him. He ceased his work, and entered into conversation with the ease and politeness of nature's noblemen. His countenance was expressive of benignity and happiness. This was the botanist, traveller, and philosopher we had come to see. (Harper 1958, xxx)

William Bartram remained active until he was eighty-five; on 22 July 1823 he died moments after finishing an article on the natural history of a plant, as he rose from his desk to go into his gardens (Harper 1958, xxxv). More than half a lifetime

---

10. Rich in anthropological information about the American Indian, the work has been made more accessible to the average reader with the publication of a naturalist's edition (Harper 1958), which updates and simplifies much of the original technical terminology.

had passed since the flower hunter had sailed alone up the St.
Johns River, taking notes for his *Travels* and "studying and
contemplating the works and power of the Creator [to] learn
wisdom and understanding in the economy of nature" (Bartram [1791] 1940, 70).

SIX

~~~~~~

John McIntosh

ALTHOUGH HE SERVED FOR A TIME AS WIL-
liam Bartram's assistant, John McIntosh did not have the soul
of a botanist or even, despite Bartram's surmise, of a business-
man. John McIntosh was born to be a soldier. By 1776, two
years after he left Bartram on the St. Johns, the twenty-year-
old McIntosh was a captain in the Georgia militia, soon to be
a lieutenant colonel, fighting the British in Florida. By 1778,
when Bartram had returned to his gardens, McIntosh had become a combat hero. He brought his wife and children to live
on the St. Johns in 1791 (the year Bartram published his *Travels*), where the Spanish first appointed him lieutenant governor, later imprisoned him for treason as a rebel, and in 1796
ordered him hanged. Three governments called on him to capture Florida from the Spanish—France in 1793, England in
1797, and American patriot forces in 1812. McIntosh served
his last military duty as a general officer in the War of 1812,
at age fifty-nine.

John McIntosh was born in Darien, Georgia, in 1756.[1] His
grandfather, John McIntosh, Mor, a Protestant from Scotland,
settled Georgia with General James Oglethorpe and in 1740

1. In 1794 he said he was thirty-eight years old (Bennett 1982, 83). But com-
pare Cate (1930, 188) and Bartram (1943, 174).

fought with the general against the Spanish Catholic government at St. Augustine.[2] He was captured there, then imprisoned in Spain and released two years later.

When he was seventeen, John McIntosh joined William Bartram in Savannah in May 1773. En route to their first destination, an Indian treaty parley at Augusta, the two visited Ebenezer, Georgia, and Silver Bluff, South Carolina, settlements on the Savannah River. The parley ended on 3 June (Bartram 1943, 135, 177, 191), and Bartram wrote that McIntosh was "anxious" to set off with the surveyors to look over the lands acquired by the treaty for future white settlements (Bartram 1794, 35). On that journey, Bartram wrote that he made solitary "little excursions" around the camp "after turning out our horses and pitching camp," since not many in the party shared his interests. "Except," he went on, "when I could sometimes prevail on Mr. McAntosh to accompany me, who was my companion in this journey & whose company I was fond of, being of a lively & good disposition" (Bartram 1943, 139).

On one of those excursions, when the survey team was camped on the banks of a tributary of Georgia's Broad River, Bartram wrote, "On my return towards camp, I met my philosophic companion, Mr. McIntosh, who was seated on the bank of a rivulet, and whom I found highly entertained by a very novel and curious natural exhibition, in which I participated with high relish." The entertainment was an ongoing underwater battle between crayfish and goldfish, which Bartram described in poetic detail (Bartram 1794, 43).

On their way to explore the St. Johns River in the spring of 1774, McIntosh and Bartram stopped at Frederica, James Spalding's home on St. Simons Island, Georgia. Spalding, a merchant, was married to McIntosh's sister Margery (Huxford 1967, 5:405).[3] At St. Simons they boarded a sloop and set sail for Cumberland Island, then for Amelia Island (McInnis 1979, 86). There Mr. Egan, superintendent of Lord Egmont's hold-

2. "Mor" is a Gaelic word that means great, esteemed, or senior, usually following the last name but sometimes following the first.
3. A man with loyalist leanings, Spalding moved to Florida in the early days of the Revolution; he eventually sold his Indian trading stores there to William Panton (Coker 1976, 3, 36).

ings, took them on to visit Francis Fatio's plantation on the St. Johns, a visit that years later would prove fortuitous for McIntosh.

A little farther upstream, at Cowford, McIntosh elected to stay behind "amongst the settlements" rather than to proceed with Bartram, a decision Bartram assumed was based on the young man's ambition to get on with a more ordinary way of life (Bartram 1794, 21). Just as likely, however, it was that McIntosh found the botanist, a practicing Quaker, out of touch with the revolutionary spirit already mounting in the colonies. Perhaps he chose to express his patriotism through soldiering rather than science. In any event, within a few months of his return to Darien, McIntosh signed a document on 12 January 1775 protesting British treatment of New England colonists. His uncle, Lachlan McIntosh (later a major general with the patriots), also endorsed "the decent but firm and manly conduct of the loyal and brave people of Boston and Massachusetts Bay to preserve their liberty."

The introduction of the document is written with a heady patriotism that must have been irresistible to many young men.

In the Darien Committee.—When the most valuable privileges of a people are invaded, not only by open violence, but by every kind of fraud, sophistry, and cunning, it behooves every individual to be upon his guard, and every member of society, like beacons in a country surrounded by enemies, to give the alarm; not only when their liberties in general are attacked, but separately, lest a precedent in one may affect the whole; and to enable the collective wisdom of such people to judge of its consequences, and how far their respective grievances concern all, or should be opposed to preserve their necessary union. (Knight 1913, 771)

As colonial frustration with England grew, so did McIntosh's political activism, and on 7 January 1776 he was commissioned a captain and took command of the First Georgia Company (Cate 1930, 188; White 1855, 94). Long enough afterward for McIntosh to have risen in rank, he was ordered to the Satilla River near Fort Howe, where Indians had ambushed some patriot troops. "Lieutenant Colonel John McIntosh with the regulars from Darien repaired to the scene of the action and buried the dead; who had been scalped, and their bodies so much mangled that only a few of them were known," wrote his companion in arms Hugh McCall. "These allies of his Britannic majesty, were not satisfied with taking away the life: the bodies of the dead were ripped open with knives and the intestines strewed about the ground" (McCall [1811] 1909, 347).

During the Revolution, McIntosh served mainly as an officer in the Continental Army rather than in the militia. He was stationed for a time in Charleston, where the Southern Department of Washington's forces, the continentals, were headquartered, first under General Charles Lee, then under General Robert Howe. There he became engaged to the "light and delicate" Sarah Swinton, whose father had died in battle against the British. Miss Swinton "espoused with an almost imprudent zeal the cause of freedom, in a part of the country infested by Tories, and marauding bands of British troops." It was not a Britisher who riled McIntosh, however, but a fellow patriot, Captain Elholm, "a Polander in the American service (Lee's Legion)." When McIntosh learned that Elholm had "acted oppressively toward some of the inhabitants" of Miss Swinton's neighborhood, he challenged him to a duel. Both men were "young, resolute, active, and powerful"; it was expected to be a duel to the death (White 1855, 547).

> The hostile parties met under a large oak, the ground about which was soon cleared of every obstacle that might impede the movements of the combatants. At the word "Ready," they drew, and advancing with sharp and glittering swords, commenced the battle in good earnest, with firm hearts and sturdy arms. In a little time the right arm of Captain Elholm was nearly severed from his body, and fell powerless by his side. Here it might be supposed that the contest would cease: not so; there was but a momentary pause, for he was a proud, fearless soldier, expert with his weapon, and naturally left-handed. His sword was dexterously transferred to his left hand, which he used with great effect and the blows came so awkwardly, that they were not easily parried by his right-handed antago-

nist. Both were in a few moments disabled in such a manner that the friends present felt it proper to interfere, and end the bloody conflict. (White 1855, 547)

A little time after this duel, McIntosh brought Sarah Swinton to Georgia as his wife (White 1854, 548).

On 3 April 1778, McIntosh assumed command of the Third Georgian Regiment (Cate 1930, 188) and served on General Robert Howe's staff in operations against the British in Florida, including several skirmishes and a battle at Alligator Creek, between the St. Marys and Nassau rivers. Problems arose, however—widespread illness among the men, short supplies, conflicts between the commanding officers of the continentals and the state militia, and the loss of the strategic element of surprise. On 11 July, Lieutenant Colonel McIntosh joined in the unanimous conclusion reached by Howe's council of war that an attack on St. Augustine would be an unsound military move. Instead, the patriots drove the British from the St. Marys River and thus, they hoped, discouraged the expected British invasion of Georgia (McCall [1811] 1909, 360; Bennett 1970, 43).

The most dramatic event of McIntosh's military career came with an exchange of notes, not shots. In November 1778, the British had begun their offensive against Savannah. Colonel McIntosh was in command of a two-hundred-man force at Fort Morris, in Sunbury, Georgia (a port on the south bank of the Medway River near its mouth, in Liberty County) when on 25 November, Colonel L. V. Fuser and about five hundred British regulars surrounded the fort and sent a note to its twenty-two-year-old commander by the hand of Major Lane of the continental troops:

Sir:—You cannot be ignorant that four armies are in motion to reduce this Province. The one is [already] under the guns of your fort, and may be joined when I think proper, by Colonel Prevost, who is now at the Medway meetinghouse. The resistance you can or intend to make will only bring destruction upon this country. On the contrary, if you will deliver to me the fort which you command, lay down your arms, and remain neuter until the fate of America is determined, you shall, as well as all of the inhabitants of this parish, remain in peaceable possession of your property. Your answer, which I expect in an hour's time, will determine the fate of this country, whether it is to be laid in ashes, or remain as above proposed. I am, sir, your most obedient &c., L. V. Fuser, Colonel 60th Regiment, and Commander of his Majesty's Troops in Georgia, on his Majesty's Service. P.S.— Since this letter was closed, some of your people have been firing scattering shot about the line. I am to inform you, that if a stop is not put to such irregular proceedings, I shall burn a house for every shot so fired. (White 1855, 525)

Major Lane soon delivered McIntosh's reply to Colonel Fuser:

Sir:– We acknowledge we are not ignorant that your army is in motion to endeavour to reduce this State. We believe it entirely chimerical that Colonel Prevost is at the Meeting-house; but should it be so, we are in no degree apprehensive of danger from a junction of his army with yours. We have no property compared with the object we contend for that we value a rush [a piece of straw used to start a fire] and would rather perish in a vigorous defence than accept of your proposals. We, sir, are fighting the battles of America, and therefore disdain to remain neutral till its fate is determined. As to surrendering the fort, receive this laconic reply, "COME AND TAKE IT." Major Lane, whom I send with this letter, is directed to satisfy you with respect to the irregular, loose firing mentioned on the back of your letter. I have the honour to be, Sir, your most obedient serv't, John McIntosh, Colonel of Continental Troops. (White 1855, 525)

Unwilling to call McIntosh's bluff, the British retreated. Later, the Georgia legislature presented McIntosh a sword engraved "Come and take it" (Coulter 1947, 136).

In spite of such brave acts by the patriots, Savannah fell on 29 December to a British force of about thirty-five hundred under Colonel Campbell. Since McIntosh's commanding officer, Colonel Samuel Elbert, helped defend Savannah, McIn-

Fair Hope Plantation, McIntosh County, Georgia, last home of General John McIntosh. Courtesy Georgia Department of Archives and History.

tosh, too, was probably among the valiant eight hundred continentals and four hundred militia who fought there under General Robert Howe (Carrington 1881, 459). Not long after, Augusta and Sunbury also fell to the British. They shortly abandoned Augusta, however, and McIntosh and Colonel John Twiggs assembled some militia in that area, went downriver, and surprised an outpost of seventy men at Herbert's. There they killed and wounded several of the British regulars and militia; the rest surrendered (McCall [1811] 1909, 400).

In March 1779, General John Ashe, with fifteen hundred North Carolina militia and some Georgia continental troops, McIntosh among them, had orders to pursue the retreating British down the west side of the Savannah River after the British decided to consolidate their forces at Savannah. The patriots pitched camp at the angle of Brier Creek with the river, where the British surprised them (White 1849, 417; McIlvaine 1971, 68). In the ensuing battle, three divisions made up the patriot line, the left—with sixty continental troops and one hundred fifty militia—committed to General

Elbert and Colonel McIntosh. "The center and right fled in utmost confusion. General Elbert with the left maintained his ground with so much gallantry that the British reserve was ordered to support their right." The general held until no line of retreat remained. When he realized that "further resistance would be temerity, he ordered his gallant little band to ground their arms and surrender. Nearly the whole of his command was killed, wounded, or made prisoners" (McCall [1811] 1909, 405).

Among the prisoners was John McIntosh, whose "life was narrowly saved by the timely intrusion of Sir Anneas McIntosh, a kinsman in the opposite ranks" (Bartram 1943, 212). Apparently he remained a prisoner until late 1780, when he was exchanged for a British officer, Colonel Cruger (McCall [1811] 1909, 421).[4]

Although no information has come to light about Colonel McIntosh's movements during the rest of the war, he was probably involved in the harassing operations against the British that made up most of the military action in the South in the war's closing months. Few battles were won, but each nevertheless contributed to the ultimate defeat in 1781 of the British at Yorktown.

After the war, McIntosh found himself deeply in debt, a position especially uncomfortable in Georgia. Although Georgia was originally chartered in part to aid imprisoned debtors, by the late eighteenth century debtors could be isolated from society under house arrest. Many indebted Georgians moved to Florida, where Spain (having regained the peninsula from England at the end of the Revolution) was offering land to new settlers (Patrick 1954, 50; Snodgrass 1969c, 23). By then a major in the Georgia militia (Cate 1930, 234), McIntosh served in one session of the Georgia legislature before joining the exodus.

In April 1791, John and Sarah McIntosh came with their children to the St. Johns River at the cowford that the Spanish called San Nicolas (Patrick 1954, 50). They acquired thousands of acres of land on both sides of the river, but their main plan-

4. Although McCall, writing in 1784, placed the exchange in 1779, another source dates Cruger's capture as 1780 (Boatner 1966, 692).

tation lay on the south bank, immediately east of Francis Fatio's indigo plantation. They named this cotton plantation Cerro Fuente, Spring Hill.[5] Almost immediately, the Spanish government appointed McIntosh lieutenant governor for the St. Johns district (*Papeles de Cuba*, 20; Bennett 1982, 13), and in 1792 it called upon him and other prominent citizens to make a census of East Florida's natural resources (Miller 1979, 96). The Spanish authorities counted McIntosh, with his grand military record, a stabilizing influence in the potentially explosive district.

Frustration ran deep among the settlers of East Florida. Supplies and all sorts of purchases were hard to come by. Many settlers felt that Panton, Leslie and Company held an unfair monopoly on the Indian trading business. East Florida's decadent colonial government with its associated religious strictures stood in disheartening contrast to the democratic, progressive spirit of the young United States. Immigrants entering the colony had to make certain commitments, among them a promise to eschew the public practice of any religion except Catholicism. The river valleys of the St. Johns and the St. Marys and the lands between were popular settling places for new arrivals from the north, and as time went on settlers there grew more restive and more openly critical of Spanish rule.

McIntosh was not immune to these frustrations. Familiar with a government open to suggestions, he found that even when the Florida governor sympathized with his views, Madrid seemed always to rule against substantial improvements. A case in point was a petition McIntosh signed along with such other administration stalwarts as Juan McQueen and Andrew Atkinson. Dated 10 January 1793, the petition pointed out how economic matters had deteriorated under Spanish rule and complained about the scarcity of supplies and the Panton, Leslie monopoly. Even though the Florida governor sympathized somewhat with the complaints, authorities in Madrid made no substantial changes.[6]

5. The McIntosh plantation on the north bank embraced much of the land that today is downtown Jacksonville. Most of the material in this chapter for the period 1791 to 1796 is condensed from Bennett 1982.

6. *Santo Domingo*, 22, enclosed in Quesada to Gardoqui, 10 January 1793, St. Augustine.

Disappointment at rebuffs of this kind may have been behind McIntosh's decision to align himself with the rebels who
sought to wrest the government of East Florida from Spain,
among them some of McIntosh's closest friends and comrades
in arms from the Revolution. Their natural ally was France,
at war with Spain in 1793 and eager to wield more influence
in America by creating French-oriented republics out of Spanish colonies. Florida, ripe for rebellion, was a good place to
start. The new Republic of France commissioned Samuel
Hammond, a Savannah merchant, a "Colonel in command of
the Revolutionary Legion of the Floridas," the commander
in chief of the projected assault on East Florida. One of
McIntosh's friends, Hammond hoped to see his trading house
succeed Panton, Leslie and Company in Florida (Murdoch
1951, 15, 157). A similar French commission went to General
Elijah Clark, who had been with McIntosh in the 1778 Florida
invasion (Murdoch 1951, 114).

McIntosh assisted Hammond's efforts from a very early
date. In June 1793, Hammond wrote to him, "Nothing could
give me more pleasure in this world than to be lodged or established in the same neighborhood as you with our families together and in good health" (*Papeles de Cuba*, 81). Before the
close of the year, McIntosh advised Captain Richard Lang of
the St. Marys frontier to retain his Spanish militia commission
on the St. Marys until the new government came into power.
Then Lang could carry on for the new government because,
according to a statement by George Arons, McIntosh assumed
that Florida "very shortly . . . would be free and independent
and then [Lang] would command this river and McIntosh the
St. Johns" (*Papeles de Cuba*, 67).[7] Like Thomas Jefferson and
many other American leaders at the time, McIntosh believed
that any Florida republic that might come into being would
soon join the United States.

When the Spanish authorities uncovered the rebellion early
in 1794, they seized McIntosh and other supporters and

7. Arons, a resident of Florida but formerly of Georgia, had been told by
a friend in Georgia of the impending plans for a French revolution in Florida
"so that Arons could protect his property; that this information was given by
his neighbor in gratitude for Arons having saved his life some years before"
(Bennett 1982, 53–54).

brought legal proceedings against them. After a year in a Havana prison, McIntosh was returned to Florida and freed without further penalty because the evidence showed him guilty only of giving moral support to the rebels, not of performing any treasonous act. Sarah McIntosh had worked to secure his release with help from President Washington (Bennett 1982, 136–47). Even the McIntoshes' neighbor, Francis Fatio, a loyal Spaniard, had petitioned in McIntosh's behalf (Bennett 1982, 174–75).

The rebellion simmered with no further spectacular event until 29 June 1795, when, under the direction of General Elijah Clark at the St. Marys River, Richard Lang captured Juana, a small fort six miles north of the St. Johns (Murdoch 1951, 84, 85). Less than a fortnight later, on 10 July, Lang, McIntosh, and others captured San Nicolas, the Spanish fort on the south bank of the river at the cowford, shouting cries for liberty and bearing the French Republican flag. The Spanish authorities recaptured the fort within a few days and started criminal proceedings against the rebels, while McIntosh, Lang, Clark, and most of the other leaders fled back across the St. Marys. The Spaniards proceeded to try the rebels in absentia and in 1796 sentenced McIntosh and others to have ropes placed around their necks, to be dragged by the tail of a horse around the plaza in St. Augustine, and there to be hanged on a gallows; at the end of three days their bodies were to be quartered and their heads and arms displayed in the vicinity of San Nicolas to serve as a warning to others. In fact no one was executed, and at the turn of the century the Spanish authorities pardoned those who still lived in East Florida (Miller 1978, 185; Bennett 1982, 172–204). By then, a weak Spanish colonial government feared that imposing penalties would more likely precipitate new rebellion than deter it.[8]

John McIntosh, however, had returned to southeastern Georgia for good. A successful soldier-planter, for the next fifteen years most of his energies went into agriculture, al-

8. Details of what happened in the 1790s on the shores of the St. Johns River continue to come to light as many documents of the period are only now being translated from the Spanish. At the University of Florida, for example, work is proceeding on a "Calendar of the Spanish Holdings of the P.K. Yonge Library of Florida History."

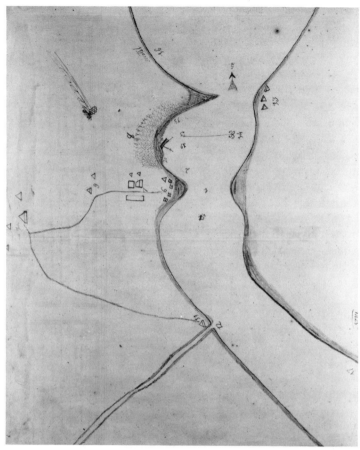

San Nicolas battle map, 1795, showing land now part of downtown Jackson-ville. B294P12, p. 1425, reel 129, East Florida Papers, Library of Congress.

though he continued to serve in the Georgia militia and per-form various civic duties. He was appointed security for two estates: on 15 December 1795 for the estate of his brother-in-law James Spalding, and in 1796 for that of his friend and com-rade in arms Christopher Hillary. He served on a grand jury, got involved in politics, and often made social and business trips to Savannah (Cate 1930, 187–260 passim).

In 1797, British authorities offered McIntosh the command of an expeditionary force to be raised in Georgia for the capture of Florida. Because Britain had declared war on Spain in 1796, she had strategic and economic motives for seizing both Florida and Louisiana (Wright 1966, 279). McIntosh first assured himself that a captured Florida would soon belong to the United States, then accepted the British offer. Among the many details agreed on was the capture of Amelia Island for a base of operations as a first step. Eventually, however, England abandoned the project ("Memorandum of 1797").

Two years later, Sarah McIntosh died and was buried on St. Simons Island. In 1804, McIntosh served in the Georgia Assembly representing Glynn County (Cate 1930, 228).

A secret act approved by the U.S. government on 15 January 1811 would eventually draw McIntosh back into active military service. The act authorized the president "to take possession of and occupy all or any part of the territory lying east of the river Perdido and south of the state of Georgia and the Mississippi territory, in case an arrangement has been or shall be made with the local authority of said territory for delivering up the possession of the same, or any part thereof, to the United States or in the event of an attempt to occupy the said territory or any part thereof by any foreign government" (Miller 1918, 5). President Madison signed the act into law and appointed General George Matthews of the Georgia militia and U.S. Indian agent John McKee to see whether annexation might be achieved peacefully.

Based on rumors he had heard, Matthews initially believed that the governors of East and West Florida would allow him to take over their provinces without resistance. Fortunately, he did some preliminary investigation and asked George Atkinson, a prominent Spanish militia officer, how Governor Enrique White might greet such a request. "As sure as you open your mouth to White on the subject," Atkinson shot back, "you will die in chains in Morro Castle [in Havana, Cuba], and all the devils in Hell can't save you!" (Patrick 1954, 41). Although Matthews justified his actions as supporting U.S. government efforts to collect maritime spoliation claims acknowledged by Spanish authorities (Patrick 1954, 151), the Florida governors had not been authorized to accede to any such arrangements.

At this juncture, Matthews and Indian agent McKee were

probably correct when they interpreted their task to be to organize rebellion in Florida and turn over the land taken by the rebels to the U.S. government. Under the leadership of McIntosh's cousin John Houston McIntosh, U.S. troops did take the land from the St. Marys south to St. Augustine—the ominous presence of U.S. warships in the harbor persuaded the Spanish garrison at Fernandina to yield that town to the rebel Patriots on 17 March 1812 without a shot being fired (Patrick 1954, 96–98). Four days later, across the St. Johns from Cowford, three of the Spanish soldiers at Fort San Nicolas surrendered, and the rest of the garrison fled to St. Augustine (Patrick 1954, 102).

The Patriot troops now assembled for an attack on St. Augustine and on 12 April seized Moosa, a small, old fort only two and a half miles from the city. As at Fernandina, the Patriots surrendered the newly occupied land to the United States, this being the sole purpose of their transitional government. Matthews ran up the American flag and turned over possession of the fort to the U.S. troops. Doubtful about taking St. Augustine, the military leaders on the scene called on Major General John McIntosh of the Georgia militia for his advice. McIntosh arrived at camp on 17 April 1812 and promptly estimated their chances of success as minimal. Still, the Patriot forces insisted that he serve as their commander in chief. McIntosh accepted and tendered his resignation from the Georgia militia.

Soon afterward, John Houston McIntosh chaired a committee of three—Zephaniah Kingsley, William Craig, and Buckner Harris—to put on a drive for recruits. Although some new recruits did sign on, the Patriots never took St. Augustine. On 4 April, even before McIntosh arrived at the Patriots' camp, Secretary of State James Monroe had repudiated not only the actions of General Matthews but the entire Florida operation. A British plot to foment rebellion in the United States had just been found out, and anti-British passions were running high, a reaction that made untenable a similar course of action by the United States in Florida. The project was abandoned, a move McIntosh found unjust. On 1 May he wrote Georgia's Governor David Mitchell, Matthews's replacement, "I think the government can never abandon [the Florida Patriots] to inevitable ruin, after being in some degree invited to this revolution" (Patrick 1954, 123). To a lesser extent, the East Florida rebellion did stay alive until April 1814, when President Monroe repudiated any U.S. support for continued revolutionary activities in Florida (Patrick 1954, 282).[9]

While McIntosh concerned himself with the East Florida rebels, the elections of 1810 had sent to Washington a new brand of young congressmen christened War Hawks, mostly southerners and westerners with territorial ambitions for the United States in the Northwest and Florida. Among their leaders were Henry Clay and John C. Calhoun, men who bore fierce resentments against England for U.S. economic injuries and humiliations arising from the Napoleonic wars and for the way England encouraged Indian hostilities in the Northwest. The War Hawks hoped to use a war with England to secure Florida from Spain, an English ally. Certainly the anti-British sentiment they stirred up contributed to the declaration of war on 18 June 1812, although the war's ostensible purpose was to end the oppressive maritime practices England had adopted during the Napoleonic wars, such as blockading ports and impressing seamen.

With war looming, Major General John McIntosh's resignation from the Georgia militia had been turned down. He was first called to command three infantry regiments and an artillery battalion defending Savannah, but when the British threatened the Gulf coast, "McIntosh with his gallant Georgians marched a thousand miles to the defense of Mobile" (Gamble [1794] 1923, 20). As General Andrew Jackson pushed on to New Orleans, he called upon his old friend General McIntosh to command the troops in the eastern sector.[10] In McIntosh's headquarters at Mobile on 22 February 1815, his aide-de-camp noted this for the record and quoted the general on the British: "Although they have made the science of war their study; yet they have been uniformly beaten when they have contended with us on equal terms" (Louisiana Historical

9. Chapter 7 includes details on the progress of the Patriot rebellion after May 1812.
10. For a discussion of McIntosh's activities in the War of 1812, see Owsley (1981, 135, 173–75).

Association). At fifty-nine, McIntosh received his highest rank in the U.S. military.

Technically, the war had ended by this time, with the signing of the Treaty of Ghent on 24 December 1814. Not until two weeks later, on 8 January, did Jackson and his troops take New Orleans in the U.S. army's most spectacular victory of the war. Had news of the signing been further delayed, the strength of the British forces arrayed against McIntosh at Mobile might have forced him to try another Sunbury bluff.

McIntosh spent the last decade of his life running his plantation, Fair Hope, in McIntosh County, Georgia, with his second wife, Agnes, the widow of his longtime friend Christopher Hillary. When he died in 1826, the editor of the *Georgia* eulogized him in language typical of the romantic extravagance of the times but moving, nonetheless: "Noble soul!" he wrote of the old soldier, "How the spirit of Washington will greet thee!" (Gamble [1794] 1923, 22).

SEVEN

~~~~~~

Zephaniah Kingsley

THE OWNER OF PLANTATIONS UP AND
down the St. Johns River in the first half of the nineteenth century, Zephaniah Kingsley was a man of contradictions. A peace-loving Quaker, he supported Florida's Patriot rebellion in 1812. At the same time that he smuggled slaves and later served in the territorial legislature and as a justice of the peace, he was a bigamist whose wives were all women of color. He was a slaveholder whom his neighbors branded an abolitionist because of his writings and speeches on the civil rights of blacks. With the earnings of plantations worked by black slaves, he built a colony in Haiti for free blacks. "It was altogether vain to argue with him about fixed principles of right and wrong," an interviewer wrote toward the end of Kingsley's life. "One might as well fire small shot at the hide of a rhinoceros" (Child 1970, 158).

Zephaniah was the second of eight children born to Zephaniah Kingsley and the former Isabella Johnstone, a British noblewoman. The family claimed some prominent members. The young Zephaniah's maternal grandparents were Lady Katherine and Sir William Johnstone, the Marquis of Arundel and Earl of Hartfell. His youngest sister, Martha Kingsley McNeill, would have a daughter who would marry George Washington Whistler and model for paintings by their artist son, James McNeill Whistler. At the time Zephaniah was born in Scotland on 4 December 1765, his mother's uncle, George Johnstone, was the British governor of West Florida. When Zephaniah was eight, his family migrated from England to Charleston, where his father became a successful merchant. Banished in 1782 on the grounds that he had been among the "Petitioners to the British Commandant of Charles Town to be armed as loyal militia," the senior Kingsley fled with his family to Canada. There he became a substantial landholder, merchant, and one of the founders of the University of New Brunswick (May 1945, 145–59; Snodgrass 1969b, 74, 82).[1]

Meanwhile, the young Zephaniah Kingsley traveled and pursued business ventures in the British Isles, Africa, the West Indies, and the Americas. Around the turn of the century he was a coffee importer and lived in Santo Domingo at one time for nearly a year, during which time he "often travelled alone, and on horseback . . . through woods and over mountains, with my saddle bags loaded with specie to buy coffee" (Kingsley 1834, 18).

In 1803, when Kingsley was thirty-eight, he spent a short time in St. Augustine. Later that year he returned to Florida with his wife, Anna Madgigene Jai. They settled at Laurel Grove plantation at the mouth of Doctor's Inlet on the St. Johns, formerly owned by the widow of William Pengree, who had been granted the land by Spain (*American State Papers*, 4:282, 660). Anna Jai's father was said to be a chief of Madagascar, who was also rumored to have helped Kingsley procure slaves. "If you want to see beautiful specimens of the human race," Kingsley would later say, "you should see some of the native women there." Anna Jai herself he described as "a fine, tall figure, black as jet, but very handsome. She was very capable, and could carry on all the affairs of the plantation in my absence, as well as I could myself. She was affectionate and faithful, and I could trust her" (Child 1970, 156).

Of his marriage to Anna Jai, Kingsley wrote in his will (on record at the Duval County Courthouse), "Our connubial relations took place in a foreign land, where our marriage was cel-

1. Particularly on Kingsley, Sr., and his activities in Canada, see the correspondence in the Florida State Park files at Tallahassee.

ebrated and solemnized by her native African custom although
never celebrated according to the forms of Christian usage;
yet she has always been respected as my wife and as such I
acknowledge her, nor do I think that her truth, honor, integ-
rity, moral conduct, or good sense will lose in comparison with
anyone." Anna Jai was the first of at least four black women
Kingsley would marry and set up on separate plantations
along the St. Johns (Corse 1931, 115).
   Kingsley may have come to Florida at the suggestion of Don
Juan McQueen (Gold 1929, 70).[2] Certainly both knew about the
constitutional provision that would allow legislation in 1808 to
outlaw the slave trade, and both looked forward to taking full
advantage of the opportunity the new law would offer. After
the Embargo Act was enacted on 7 March 1807, McQueen
wrote to his son, "Pray do you not think great matters may
be done in the African trade from the Island of Amelia in this
Province when the door shall be shut next year by the Congress to the importation of slaves?" (Cabell and Hanna 1943,
144).
   Slave trading laid the foundation for Kingsley's business
empire. From African chiefs he bought prisoners taken in tribal combat. His men picked up the prisoners at Reuter's, his
partner's base camp on the banks of the Congo, and loaded
them on his fleet of schooners. The ships sailed to Brazil, the
West Indies, and the Spanish Floridas, where the slaves were
trained and sold or smuggled across the St. Marys for sale in
the United States. Because of the excellent training Kingsley's
slaves received on his plantations, they always brought pre-
mium prices (Cabell and Hanna 1943, 164).
   Kingsley had fond memories of the slaves at Laurel Grove
before the 1812 rebellion, and wrote about them years later:

   About twenty-five years ago, I settled a plantation on St. Johns
   River, in Florida, with about fifty new African negroes, many
   of whom I brought from the coast myself. They were mostly

2. McQueen, a loyal Spanish subject originally from South Carolina, held
extensive lands in Florida. His beautiful 1791 plantation house on Fort George
Island still stands and will become a national park facility. He participated
in the combat leadership which expelled the 1795 revolutionaries (including
McIntosh) (Bennett 1982, 126, 185, 191, 195).

fine young men and women, and nearly in equal numbers. I never interfered with their connubial concerns, nor domestic affairs, but let them regulate these after their own manner. I taught them nothing but what was useful, and what I thought would add to their physical and moral happiness. I encouraged as much as possible dancing, merriment, and dress, for which Saturday afternoon and night, and Sunday morning, were dedicated; and, after allowance, their time was usually employed in hoeing their corn, and getting a supply of fish for the week. Both men and women were very industrious. Many of them made twenty bushels of corn to sell, and they vied with each other in dress and dancing, and as to whose wife was the finest and prettiest. They were perfectly honest and obedient, and appeared quite happy, having no fear but that of offending me; and I hardly ever had occasion to apply other correction than shaming them. If I exceeded this, the punishment was quite light, for they hardly ever failed in doing their work well. My object was to excite their ambition and attachment by kindness: not to depress their spirits by fear and punishment. I never allowed them to visit, for fear of bad example, but encouraged the decent neighboring people to participate in their weekly festivity, for which they always provided an ample entertainment themselves, as they had an abundance of hogs, fowls, corn and all kinds of vegetables and fruits. They had nothing to conceal from me, and I had no suspicion of any crime in them to guard against. Perfect confidence, friendship and good understanding reigned between us; they increased rapidly. (Kingsley 1834, 21)

Throughout his life Kingsley believed that such a condition as good slavery was possible. "The idea of slavery," he wrote in his late sixties, "when associated with cruelty and injustice, is revolting to every philanthropic mind; but when that idea is associated with justice and benevolence, slavery, commonly so called, easily amalgamates with the ordinary conditions of life. . . . The condition of slaves may be equally happy and more independent of the ordinary evils of life than that of the common class of whites denominated free." Not surprisingly, Kingsley held that benevolent slavery benefited not only the slave but also the state and society. Compared to "the ordinary class of laboring whites," the work of slaves "is far more productive . . . [and] they yield more support and benefit to the State." In fact, "the Slave or Patriarchal System of Society (so often commiserated as a subject of deep regret) which constitutes the bond of social compact of the Southern seaboard of the United States, is better adapted for strength, durability, and independence, than any other state of society hitherto adopted" (Kingsley 1834, 3).

During his early years on the St. Johns, Kingsley shared the leadership of northeast Florida with George J. F. Clarke of Amelia Island, like Kingsley a wealthy planter and slaveholder with a black common-law wife. In the years leading up to 1812, according to Clarke, in Florida and particularly in Fernandina, "every man was making money hand over hand, as fast as he could; and in consequence of the restrictive measures of the American government, the trade of the United States with all the world, except Spain, centered at Fernandina." Kingsley concurred, observing that "the country was in a very flourishing state when the [Patriot] revolution commenced" (U.S. Congress, 17, 24).

That revolution was triggered in 1811 by a secret U.S. act authorizing the president to "take possession of and occupy all or any part of the territory lying east of the river Perdido and south of the state of Georgia" (Miller 1918, 5). On 18 March 1812, Kingsley reluctantly became involved in the resulting Patriot rebellion led by General George Matthews. The Patriots took Kingsley from Laurel Grove to their camp at Cowford at two o'clock in the morning and threatened to have his property seized if he failed to support their cause. He signed their "act of independence" on the condition that "he should go home and be protected against the Indians" (U.S. Congress, 23). As another result of this meeting, Kingsley's plantation, San José, on the east bank of the St. Johns just north of Goodby's Lake, became Fort New Hope, a base camp for troops assembling to attack St. Augustine. (Kingsley later renamed the plantation New Hope.) The zenith of the rebellion came soon afterward, when a more willing Kingsley along with John Houston McIntosh, William Craig, and Buckner Harris managed to sign up some new recruits. The Patriots' effort was doomed, however. By 4 April the U.S. government had re-

Martha Kingsley McNeill, sister of Zephaniah Kingsley, 1834, portrait by Samuel Waldo and William Jewett. Courtesy Wadsworth Atheneum Museum, Hartford, Connecticut.

placed General Matthews with Georgia's Governor David Mitchell, who was ordered to take a less aggressive stance. But the Patriots refused to concede defeat.[3] On 10 July, Kingsley was one of fifteen delegates elected to draft a Patriot constitution, which was promptly accepted. A 25 July election sent representatives to a legislative council, which met at Kingsley's Laurel Grove. The council elected John H. McIntosh director of the Territory of East Florida and agreed on a central objective: to acquire the land of East Florida and turn it over to the United States (Patrick 1954, 166). (John H. McIntosh later sold Kingsley his plantation house on Fort George Island.)

The Indians, by now spoiling for a fight, let the Patriots know that they would be happy to join them against the Spanish. Kingsley and McIntosh, however, feared all Indians on the warpath, even allies, and determined to urge them to stay out of the war. The night Kingsley was at Picolata engaged in this tactless parley, the Indians stole his horse and rode off to offer their services to the Spanish (U.S. Congress, 23, 24). East Florida's Spanish governor, Sebastian Kindelan, was quick to recognize an advantage. He told the Indians the Patriots would take their lands and warned their allies—runaway slaves—that the Patriots would condemn them to slavery again. On 26 July the Indians and blacks launched a war against the Patriots, with all plantations and settlements considered disloyal to Spain as fair game. By 9 August, without a single Spanish soldier committed to an offensive, Kindelan was able to announce that the investment of St. Augustine had been broken (Patrick 1954, 194).

At Kingsley's Laurel Grove that August, the Indians and blacks captured slaves and burned many buildings (Patrick 1954, 186).[4] The battle was evidently not one-sided, however. A letter in the 28 October edition of the Charleston *Courier* reported that "Kingsley's house is handsomely decorated with Indian scalps" (Patrick 1954, 207). On 15 August, Abraham

3. See chapter 6 for details on the Patriots' rebellion up to May 1812.
4. Among the plantations burned out was Francis Fatio, Jr.'s New Switzerland. The family fled by boat. "Many shots were fired at us," a daughter later recorded, "and I have not yet, after the lapse of seventy years, lost the recollection of the balls falling into the river near us" (L'Engle 1888, 21).

Befsent wrote Governor Mitchell that "the Indians have made several attacks on Kingsley's premises and have consumed all his buildings except his dwelling house, which he defended with about seven men and repulsed the savages. He lost three negroes killed & twenty-six carried off " (Georgia, Creek Indians file). Before the revolution subsided, the dwelling house at Laurel Grove was burned to the ground and all the cattle stolen (Williams [1837] 1962, 200). Kingsley later wrote about his slaves' loyalty during one of the attacks:

> A war party of Seminole Indians attacked the plantation in my absence; caught, bound, and carried off, or killed, forty of [my slaves], whose reluctance in going with the invaders may be easily imagined from the following circumstance. The wife of a young man they had tied and were driving off [believed] that her husband, who was too strong to be handled and who had his young child in his arms, might follow; but this he absolutely refused, handing over the child to his wife, and saying that she knew best how to take care of it, but that his master should never say that he was a runaway negro; upon which the Indian shot him, and he died the next day. (Kingsley 1834, 21)

The threat posed against the institution of slavery by the Indian–runaway slave alliance in Florida encouraged Georgia and Tennessee to raise volunteer troops during the last half of 1812 to reinforce the Patriots, thus bolstering the appealing objective of supplanting Spanish colonialism with a new democracy (Patrick 1954, 225). The U.S. Army continued to support the Patriot cause and late in the year sent Colonel Thomas Adam Smith with U.S. troops down the east bank of the St. Johns to Kingsley's New Hope plantation. There Kingsley's flatboat carried them across the river to join forces with the Tennessee volunteers who had arrived in early February 1813. Further reinforced by men supplied by Kingsley, the joint force attacked the Indians in the Alachua area, who proved to be elusive. In over a month of combat the soldiers destroyed hundreds of Indian houses and collected scores of horses and cattle but killed only twenty Indians. The Tennesseans left soon afterward, although the U.S. troops stayed on. On 9 April 1813, Zephaniah Kingsley and other Patriot supporters petitioned the newest U.S. commissioner for the settlement of Florida's border problems, General Thomas Pinckney, who had succeeded Governor Mitchell. "Under the appelation of Patriots of whom we were a part," the signers declared they spoke "for themselves and the whole population of the St. Johns River," who were "relying on the faith and resources of the United States."[5] The petition specified that General Matthews, then U.S. commissioner, had urged the Patriots to revolt and that they now needed protection from the Indian allies of Spain. It also mentioned "black troops introduced from foreign countries," a reference to English black troops in ships offshore. This reference was no doubt intended to trigger the provision in the secret congressional act of 1811 which called for aggressive action when the threat of foreign troops in Florida became apparent (*Territorial Papers of Florida*, 12). In spite of the petition, the U.S. troops under Colonel Smith left Florida on 6 May 1813. Soon afterward, with a price of $1,000 on his scalp set by the Spanish governor, John Houston McIntosh fled the province.

The withdrawal of U.S. troops left East Florida vulnerable to every kind of outlawry. As George J. F. Clarke would testify in one of Kingsley's land litigation cases years later, "The insurrection commenced in 1812; threw the whole province into a general ferment. . . . The intermediate scuffling and fighting between the Indians and the white plundering parties about their cattle kept most parts of the province in a very uninviting, and many parts, dangerous state to all efforts of industry, and the whole western side of St. Johns river, from its proximity to such cenes the most effected by these evils" (Superior Court of East Florida, 17, 44). Stealing Indian cattle and selling them across the St. Marys became a popular way to earn one's living. Kingsley, who by this time sought only to survive with as much of his property as possible, continued to smuggle slaves northward. Captain John H. Elton on 15 November 1817 described for Secretary of the Navy B. W. Crowninshield the methods commonly used to smuggle slaves across the St. Marys: "Small boats are permitted to pass and

5. The ancestors of many families well known in Florida today signed the petition, among them Hartleys, Bardens, and Bowdens.

repass; as they are rowed by slaves they can smuggle one or two at a time without detection. Another mode of smuggling is that the law makes no provision how to consider boats of less than five tons" (Message from the President 1817, 39).

Of the Patriot leaders only Buckner Harris remained in the fray. With about a dozen men, he threatened to destroy the property of any Floridian who accepted the Spanish governor's offer of pardon. After electing Harris "Director of the District of Elatchaway [now Alachua] of the Republic of East Florida," the small band beat out loyalist forces at Waterman's Bluff on 8 August 1813. Then, instead of taking nearby Fernandina as he might have done, Harris turned southwest, back to Alachua lands. In a letter to Governor Mitchell about these actions, Harris wrote that the Indians were still on the warpath and had attacked Kingsley's Laurel Grove plantation and taken his "black wife and his two children" (Patrick 1954, 272). Not until nearly a year later, when Indians killed Harris on 5 May 1814, did all organized rebellion end (Patrick 1954, 282).

Adding to the general disorder and anxiety of the time was the British occupation of Cumberland Island on 11 January 1815, an operation of the War of 1812. Substantial numbers of blacks among their troops, including recently enlisted runaway slaves, touched off the fear common among plantation owners of a "war of color." Such a war, Kingsley later wrote, would "of all wars be the most dangerous . . . because we naturally and unavoidably (under our present policy) contain within us the materials of our own dissolution; and nine tenths of all our present white friends would at least laugh at our absurd indiscretion." (Perhaps this belief was part of the reasoning behind Kingsley's opinion that the laws regulating slavery were "entirely founded on terror.") The black troops in 1815 joined their British fellows in pillaging the little town of St. Marys, Georgia, an event that fired Kingsley's imagination: "Whoever was so unlucky as to see, on Cumberland Island . . . the magical transformation of his own negroes, whom he left in the field but a few hours before, into regular soldiers, of good discipline and appearance . . . could not help figuring to himself the consequences had there been a larger force able to maintain a position on the main[land], with any ulterior object of conquest in view. . . . Where would they have stopped or what could have stopped them?" (Kingsley 1834, 17–18). Anarchy now threatened northeastern Florida, where Spanish rule remained weak and unpopular. The governor's solution for the land between the St. Marys and the St. Johns, unique in Spanish colonial history, was to install a republican government with local leaders. As his representatives, in the summer of 1816 he appointed Kingsley, George J. F. Clarke, and Henry Yonge to bring the new government into being. Together with the inhabitants of northeast Florida, the three met at Waterman's Bluff across the river from St. Marys and divided the territory of about two hundred families into three districts: Upper St. Marys, Lower St. Marys, and Nassau. (Amelia Island, with its Spanish garrison at Fernandina, remained under royal control. About two hundred people lived in the fortified town.) The group accepted a constitution similar to Georgia's, provided a magistrate court and company of militia for each district, and elected all officials on the spot. Clarke became chief executive officer (Davis 1928, 12). The new government, under the name Northern Division of East Florida, managed most of its own affairs. Although the government decided that stealing Indian cattle and slave smuggling were activities outside its jurisdiction, some order was restored.

In 1817, Kingsley bought John Houston McIntosh's Fort George plantation, which McIntosh had fled in 1813 and where Kingsley had lived since Laurel Grove had been destroyed by Indians.[6] He installed Anna Jai Kingsley, his principal wife, in the tabby plantation house there, and next to it he ensconced himself in the larger frame dwelling, a token bow to the antimiscegenation laws.[7] An article published the year before Kingsley's death in 1843 reported that "a traveller,

6. McIntosh had bought the Fort George plantation in 1803 from Juan McQueen, granted it in 1792. McQueen is credited with building the beautiful turn-of-the-century tabby plantation house that today graces the island's northern tip in Kingsley Plantation State Park (Snodgrass 1969b, 5:80) and for the possibly earlier construction of the more imposing frame building just north of the tabby structure (*Florida Times-Union*, 4 April 1988). The tabby building contained the kitchen for the big house.

7. Some area writers continue to respect the fiction of Kingsley's bachelorhood. "His family, including his sister Martha McNeill, his niece, Anna McNeill Whistler from the North, and his sister Isabella, married to George Gibbs,

Zephaniah Kingsley's plantation house on Fort George Island.

writing from Florida, stated that he visited a planter, whose coloured wife sat at the head of the table, surrounded by healthy and handsome children. That the parlour was full of portraits of African beauties, to which the gentleman drew his attention with much exulation" (Child 1970, 154). The interviewer asked Kingsley if he were the planter referred to. He replied:

"I have no doubt that I am the man. I always thought and said, that the coloured race were superior to us, physically and morally. They are more healthy, have more graceful forms, softer skins, and sweeter voices. They are more docile and affectionate, more faithful in their attachments, and less prone to mischief, than the white race. If it were not so, they could not have been kept in slavery."

"It is a shameful and a shocking thought," said [the interviewer], "that we should keep them in slavery by reason of their very virtues."

---

and their descendants, were entertained at 'the Homestead' where he lived alone" (Watt 1968, 84).

"It is so, ma'am; but, like many other shameful things, it is true." (Child 1970, 155)

Another of Kingsley's wives, Munsilna McGundo, lived with their daughter, Fatima, at the opposite end of Fort George Island, where the tabby walls of their house still stand (May 1945, 155). Other wives and children Kingsley acknowledged in his will (on record at the Duval County Courthouse in Jacksonville) were "Flora H. Kingsley of Camp New Hope, also Sara Murphy's mulatto child Micanopy now in Hayti."

All his days in Florida, Kingsley would fight for the rights of children and families of mixed blood. In a treatise published in his last decade he wrote of the futility of "our old southern politicians" trying to regulate human emotion: "The iniquity [of mixing the races] has its origin in a great instinctive universal and immutable law of nature, legislation, by the aged, against such an alleged crime as propagation in youth, would be hopeless, and like the story of the King of Arabia, who, after destroying his appetite by excess and gluttony, made a law forbidding, under a severe penalty, that any of his subjects should be hungry" (Kingsley 1834, 20).

In addition to his plantation on Fort George, over the years Kingsley came to own many of the most beautiful sites on the St. Johns—St. Johns Bluff, New Hope, San José, and Beauclerc in what is today Duval County, Drayton's Island on the upper St. Johns, a town residence in Fernandina, and White Oak plantation on the St. Marys.[8] In later years Kingsley would plead in a case before the U.S. Supreme Court for 16,000 acres next to his Laurel Grove plantation, deeded him by a conditional land grant of 1816, his attorney's argument being that Kingsley had not started building the mill required by the grant because of the turbulent times. "The country of East Florida was in a disturbed state from the year of 1812 until the year 1815 or 1816," went one piece of testimony,

8. Kingsley willed the Beauclerc plantation to his nephew, Charles McNeill. McNeill's sister, best known as Whistler's mother, paid occasional lengthy visits to the log plantation house where she tutored Zephaniah Kingsley's grandnephews (James R. Ward, 13 May 1979, "Whistler's Mother on the St. Johns River," [Jacksonville] *Florida Times-Union.*

"particularly [in the St. Johns area]; . . . in the year 1817 it was again disturbed by the expedition under McGregor in consequence of which the troops stationed at St. Nicholas Garrison on the St. Johns river was withdrawn by the Spanish government and that part of the country was left without any protection" (*United States v. Zephaniah Kingsley*, 20).

Although Kingsley lost his case, the testimony was accurate. Neither the Northern Division of East Florida militia nor the Spanish regular troops could stop Sir Gregor McGregor and his men, under Venezuelan and other flags, from wresting the area from Spanish rule (Davis 1928, 20, 21). McGregor expected to create a republic which the United States would then annex. Disillusioned when no substantial assistance was forthcoming, McGregor sailed away about the time Luis Aury, a privateer, was unfurling the Mexican flag over northeast Florida to herald the birth of yet another revolutionary government. This was evidently the last straw for newly elected President James Monroe, who invoked the provisions of the secret act of 1811 and on 12 November 1817 sent U.S. troops into the area. On 23 December, Aury ran down the Mexican flag, and the U.S. flag went up in its stead. Federal troops remained at Amelia Island until 1819. General Andrew Jackson wrote the president on 1 January 1818 that he could take Florida in sixty days if given the signal. The signal was given by a third party, and Jackson entered West Florida with thousands of volunteers ostensibly to pursue belligerent Indians in a war now called the Seminole War of 1817–18. One result of the U.S. troops' presence in East and West Florida, according to later court testimony, was that the Indians were driven "in numerous and scattered parties down through the eastern and southern part of [the Northern Division of East Florida] to the general danger of the whole" (*United States v. Zephaniah Kingsley*, 44). Unable to maintain order in her own territory, Spain finally ceded Florida to the United States on 18 February 1818.

In 1821, after being criticized by leadership in Washington for violating international law, Jackson was rewarded by being appointed Florida's first American governor, and the following year the principal town on the St. Johns, Cowford, renamed itself Jacksonville in his honor (Snodgrass 1969a, 5:37–41; Ward 1982, 122; Bennett 1987). Across the river, the Spanish Fort San Nicolas became a memory.

Secure at last under a dependable government, Zephaniah Kingsley not only stopped smuggling slaves across the St. Marys but threw himself into civic action. He signed petitions to create a more useful postal delivery system and to run a road south from St. Augustine to the Halifax River (Carter 1959, 23:665, 945); he served on grand juries and was appointed Fort George Island postmaster (Carter 1959, 23:828, 24:204). He spoke out for a healthy business environment without excessive taxation, for new roads, bridges, and waterways. Most of all he wanted to see humane laws enacted concerning slaves and free colored people.

On 25 November 1822, Kingsley joined fifty-one other Floridians in a memorial asking the U.S. Congress not to assent to important actions of Florida's first legislative council, which had met that year at Pensacola, the old capital of West Florida. The new taxes and other objectionable enactments such as the new court system, the memorial claimed, were oppressive and "at present unnecessary" (Carter 1959, 22:565).

The federal law creating the Territory of Florida provided that its legislative power "be vested in the Governor and in thirteen of the most fit and discreet persons of the territory," the legislative council (Carter 1959, 22:391). Among the criticisms leveled against the first council was that most of those appointed to it were newcomers to the area and even that, as the 8 June 1822 issue of the *Floridian* editorialized, "there are some of the council—certainly one—who is not a citizen and who most probably never was within the Territory." In February 1823 the council president, José Hernández, suggested to the president of the United States that Kingsley be appointed to the council's next available vacancy, a recommendation already made by Governor William P. Duval (Carter 1959, 22:616, 406).

When the second session of the Florida Legislative Council met in St. Augustine in May 1823, the *East Florida Herald* of 10 May and the *Floridian* of 21 June reported that Kingsley, among the first arrivals of the Legislative Council, officially notified the governor that the council was ready to do business. Kingsley chaired the site selection committee for Florida's permanent capital, a designation vied for by both colonial capitals, Pensacola and St. Augustine, population centers widely separated by mostly unsettled land (*Floridian*, 5 July 1823). The *Floridian* reported that Kingsley also chaired the claims committee (5 July), a committee to consider "the duties of masters of slaves and the duties of slaves and free people of color and regulations necessary for their government," and a special committee to consider the petition from the free people of color (12 July). He was a member of the maritime affairs committee (12 July) and of committees to memorialize the governor on the state of the territory, to handle contingency expenditures, and to set up the government for Fernandina (5 July). One of the first bills Kingsley introduced, which provided for county government and established county courts, also enumerated the duties of justices of the peace (12 July). During the summer of 1823, Governor Duval appointed Kingsley and ten other men justices of the peace for Duval County, a position that conferred on them both administrative and lower court judicial responsibilities (9 August). Within the scope of the justices' responsibility lay construction and repair of roads, bridges, and public buildings, local taxation, jailer appointments, mill licensure, and support of the poor and infirm (5 July).

Besides the passage of Kingsley's county government bill, by the end of the session the legislature had chosen a capital. Kingsley's committee had solved the site controversy by providing for the creation of a new city about midway between Pensacola and St. Augustine. The legislation required a commissioner from West Florida and one from East Florida to proceed to St. Marks, and from there to go north and pick a site between the Suwannee and Oclockany rivers (*Acts* 1829, 33). The spot chosen, in hilly and heavily wooded wilderness, led the *East Florida Herald* editor to ask on 21 June 1823, "Why set down in the woods? Why not suffer a population to gather first about it?"

Another significant action by the second legislative council was the territory's acceptance of all of England's common and statutory law that applied to modern times and existed as of 4 July 1776, a controversial measure passed over the governor's veto (*Acts* 1829, 111). The council also enacted bills establishing a Florida militia and providing that justices of the peace and all other courts of record would supervise arbitration proceedings (*Acts* 1829, 23, 126). From Kingsley's maritime affairs committee came a law punishing by death anyone who should "make or hold out any false lights" whereby "a vessel might be cast ashore" (*Acts* 1829, 132).

Although no comprehensive record remains of debates by members of the 1823 legislative council, both the State of Florida archives and the Bennett Collection include copies of Zephaniah Kingsley's remarkable speech to that session on the institution of slavery and the rights of man. He did not plead, in his address, to abolish slavery, a concept so economically radical that even four decades later the Emancipation Proclamation freed only selected slaves. Another assumption of Kingsley's speech was the commonly held belief that only blacks could serve as agricultural laborers in Florida because only they could withstand the climate. Kingsley acknowledged to his fellow legislators that by choosing "to disclose his sentiments upon so delicate a subject" he courted difficulties and dangers. Nevertheless, he did so choose, he said, because "liberty is but an empty name—a mere burlesque—if we fear to speak the truth" (1).[9]

Although Kingsley deplored slave trading as "hideous" and admitted his own spotted history as a smuggler, the reforms for which he argued dealt mainly with better treatment of blacks, slave or free, a practice, he suggested, that conformed not only to moral principles but also to everyone's self-interest. "Do nothing inconsistent with the Divine Law of self preservation," he said in his introduction, quoting Virgil. He pointed to the fine character and responsibility of blacks, their loyal military service in the American Revolution and more recently in protecting St. Augustine in 1812, and brushed aside as ill-founded the popular notion that even well-treated blacks were likely candidates for violent revolution.

"If merit consisted in colour," Kingsley told the legislature, "a majority prejudiced in favor of any particular shade might

9. Page numbers refer to the typescript copy of Kingsley's address housed in the Bennett Collection.

drive out or exterminate the rest to make room for their favorite complexion. This would most likely depend upon what colour they have been most used to, as custom commonly regulates our degree of prejudice" (6). He urged that slaves be treated "with justice, prudence and moderation" and suggested measures to allow them to obtain their freedom easily along with laws that would open doors for free persons of color. "Let [free blacks] go as they please, and let them come as they please, acquire property, hold it and enjoy it as they please" (6).

Kingsley in his address deplored any law opposed to "civil liberty." Florida's policy, he warned, "must be liberal and such as will meet with the approbation of the United States government and the world, without which we never can rise to consequence, or be happy in our independence" (1).

His fellow legislators were not persuaded to make the immediate and significant reforms Kingsley sought, and the *East Florida Herald* of 24 June reported that his committee on the problems of colored people was discharged on their report that they could not reach agreement. Kingsley was not reappointed to the legislature. If Kingsley's ideas went unappreciated, Kingsley himself had his backers. Legislative council president José Hernández said that "Kingsley prospered not because of the soundness of his theories, but because he was one of those rare individuals whose unusual courage, vision and adaptability and industry would have made him a leader under any other conditions" (Watt 1968, 84). The territory's delegate to the U.S. Congress in 1825, Joseph White, admired Kingsley as a "classical scholar" and disparaged his fair-weather supporter, Duval. "Kingsley," White claimed, "would consider it a degradation to be put on a footing with Governor Duval in point of intellect and education" (Carter 1959, 24:511).

His brief legislative career behind him, Kingsley managed to keep busy, mainly attending to the demands of his plantations. His crops included rice, cotton, sugar, corn, peas, potatoes, and citrus. White Oak, on the St. Marys near its juncture with the Little St. Marys, in one year netted $10,000, at that time an unusually high return for one plantation (Williams [1837] 1962, 134, 135). (Irrigation canals for the White Oak rice fields can be observed today [Johannes 1976, 7, 8].) Besides the usual crops, the Fort George Island plantation included four acres of orange groves with grafted trees (Gill and Reed 1975, 135). Kingsley was one of the first Floridians to plant large acreages in citrus and to plant varieties for their export value. His success as a planter of sugarcane was reflected in a letter from George Gibbs to Joseph Delespine, published 22 March 1823 in the *East Florida Herald* in which the White Oak plantation is discussed: "In coming south the next considerable cultivation of cane is Mr. Kingsley's, on reclaimed swamp on the Florida side of St. Mary's river, about a degree south of the Altamaha, in which he had been progressing for the last three years, increasing the quantity as he increased the seed which last year was to twenty acres; from samples of the cane which I have seen and from repeated information from himself, who had been in most and resided for years in some of the West India Islands I am convinced it had attained perfection."

In 1830 the U.S. government called on Kingsley to dig a canal from Pine Island Creek to Amelia Sound and a channel through the oyster beds at Sisters to improve the inland passage. For this work Kingsley rented from the U.S. government some slaves, seized from a salvaged Spanish ship, who were waiting to be shipped back to Africa, as required by a federal statute. The government rented them to him because of his proven ability to support slaves and direct their labors.

Kingsley continued to agitate for the rights of people of color in the face of popular sentiment and laws to the contrary. In 1833 he drew up a petition urging the U.S. Congress to repudiate recently passed Florida laws as unfair to blacks and families of mixed race. His signature was followed by those of his old friend from Fernandina, George Clarke, and ten others. Kingsley's tactful opening absolved Congress of all blame: "Your Petitioners are aware," he wrote, "that the evils of which they complain have not arisen from anything inherent in the institutions and Laws of the United States, but have their origin in the illiberal prejudices of a local government totally at variance with the liberal spirit and generous policy of the nation and age in which we live" (Carter 1959, 24:800).

Specifically, the petition attacked Florida acts that not only called for special taxes for people of color but condemned those

Shooting ducks on a north Florida rice field. From Benjamin 1878.

unable to pay to be sold into slavery for life. It also condemned a law that disenfranchised a white man suspected of having a connection with a woman of color or of attempting to marry such a woman. The petition pointed out that "however these practices may be at variance with the national prejudices of a portion of the United States they existed in the recently acquired country and are not to be extinguished at once by intolerance and persecution or any other moral or political fanaticism." Such a law, the petition charged, would break up existing families and proscribe "virtuous and sacred ties of domestic life and parental affection" (Carter 1959, 24:800).

In the following year, Kingsley published a much expanded version of his 1823 legislative address on slavery, the last of four editions of his *Treatise on the Patriarchal System of Society, as It Exists in Some Governments and Colonies in America, and in the United States, under the Name of Slavery, with Its Necessity and Advantages*. In it he praised laws in other places that made it easy to free slaves and that bestowed citizenship rights, including voting rights, on children of mixed blood. Local laws he called a "system of terror," for which he blamed the general public, pointing out that "those who enact laws to regulate slaves and free people of color, are often obliged to consult popularity rather than policy and their own good sense" (19).

"A government whose laws grant exclusive privileges to the wicked and abandoned part of its population to persecute and destroy the weak of another humble part is a government of anarchy," Kingsley wrote, strong sentiments that his own life appeared to contradict: he remained a slave owner until he died. In this treatise he reconciled the seeming contradiction by his unyielding belief in the mutual benefits for slaves and good masters. "A patriarchal feeling of affection is due to every slave from his owner," he wrote, "who should consider the slave as a member of his family, whose happiness and protection is identified with that of his own family. . . . This affection creates confidence which becomes reciprocal, and is attended with the most beneficial consequences to both. It certainly is humiliating to a proud master to reflect, that he depends on his slave even for bread to eat. But such is the fact" (23).

One section of the *Treatise* took to task the ministers who visited Kingsley's slaves and the gloomy messages they brought with them, "not from any disrespect or prejudice against any particular religious profession; but when it renders men unhappy and discontented with their condition in life, by destroying local attachment and love of country, it certainly should be rationally opposed" (22). For instance, Kingsley wrote, "It was now sinful [for the slaves] to dance, work their corn or catch fish, on a Sunday, or to eat cat fish, because they had no scales; and if they did, they were to go to a place where they would be tormented with fire and brimstone to all eternity!" (21).

The next year, 1835, brought Florida's great freeze, with unprecedented and damaging low temperatures that nearly destroyed Kingsley's orange groves, killing trees down to the roots even in his southerly upriver groves on Drayton's Island. More important than the losses of seedless and navel orange trees was the blow to the philanthropic goal Kingsley had set himself, which would dominate the remaining years of his life: a full-scale colony in Haiti where blacks would be free and where all people could reach their potential, unhampered by the discriminatory laws still prevalent in Florida and elsewhere in the United States.

In 1836, Kingsley sent his son George to Haiti to get the project under way. George settled at Cabaret, twenty-seven miles east of Porte Plate, where his father and Anna Jai joined him in October with six slaves Kingsley had freed (*Rural Code* 1838, 45, 46). Back in the United States, Kingsley wrote on 30 June 1837 to the editor of the *Christian Statesman*, a member of the philanthropic African Colonization Society whose apparent object, Kingsley wrote, was "to advance the depressed free people of color to a higher grade in the scale of civilization." Describing himself as "a planter in the South, deriving my entire subsistence from slave labor, but having a colored family and children," Kingsley explained that "motives of necessity and self-preservation have induced me to labor for a similar object to yours." He wrote of his Haitian project and of the agricultural and business success of his son, "a healthy colored man of uncorrupted morals, about thirty years of age, tolerably well educated, of very industrious habits and a native of Florida." He mentioned Haiti's natural resources, including mahogany and other valuable timbers, and observed that the European nations were establishing ties with that country. Then Kingsley came to the meat of his letter: "Is it not our best policy to . . . encourage as fast as possible the industrious and most respectable part of our free colored population, especially the agricultural part, to emigrate to that country now mostly vacant, which is within a week's sail of our own coast?" (*Rural Code* 1838, 48).

In the fall of 1837, Kingsley returned to Haiti with the freed families of George's six helpers. Two years later, he sold his Fort George plantation to his nephew Kingsley Gibbs, though he was a frequent visitor there for the remaining few years of his life (Fretwell 1984, 534). Kingsley moved his main operations to his San José plantation near Mandarin, and in 1842 he brought to Haiti from his New Hope plantation Flora Kingsley and three of their sons, Osceola, William, and Jonas. An acquaintance described Kingsley at what must have been about this time as "a small, spare man, who wore square-toed, silver-buckled shoes to the last, and was generally seen about the plantation sporting a Mexican poncho. His usual exclamation was 'Dear God Almighty!'" (Benjamin 1878, 845).

In that year of 1842, the seventy-six-year-old Kingsley pressed and won several claims, the liability for which the United States had assumed under the treaty acquiring Florida from Spain. Kingsley and his lawyer nephew Kingsley Gibbs took part in discussions at the Treasury Department in Washington on 8 December, and before the day was out, Gibbs reported, Kingsley had picked up $155,140 (Fretwell 1984, 534). Treasury Department records, however, indicate that this money was claimed for other Florida residents. For his own property damage claims, Kingsley successfully argued that the United States was liable, having encouraged the events that caused the damage by revolutionaries and Indian allies of Spain. This argument also offset the counterclaim that he himself had been a revolutionary. After his death and extensive litigation, his estate would collect $77,322 on these claims from the government (May 1945, 151–52).

In an interview the same year, Kingsley talked about Anna Jai, now firmly settled in Haiti. If the interviewer went to Haiti, Kingsley promised, Anna Jai "would give you the best in the house. You ought to go, to see how happy the human race can be. . . . My son has laid out good roads, and built bridges and mills; the people are improving, and everything is prosperous. I am anxious to establish a good school there. . . . My laborers in Haiti are not slaves. They are a kind of indentured apprentices. I gave them land, and they bind themselves to work for me. I have no power to take them away from that island; and you know very well I could not sell them there" (Child 1970, 157).

The interviewer pressed Kingsley on the slavery issue. Why did he not take all his slaves to Haiti and free them there? All their descendants, she reminded him, would be affected by his decision. Kingsley, from the perspective of forty years as a slave owner, replied, "So will all Haiti be affected, through all coming time, if I can carry out my plan." Besides, "all we can do in this world is balance evils. I want to do great things for Haiti; and in order to do them I must have money." That money, he explained, came from his Florida plantations, run on slave labor. Although it grieved him now to keep slaves, he hoped it would be for only a few more years, although he thought his heirs would probably break his will if he died before his plans were realized. When the interviewer urged him to free all his slaves immediately, he said, "I have thought that all over, ma'am; and I have settled it that I can do more good by keeping them in slavery a few years more. The best we can do in this world is balance evils judiciously" (Child 1970, 158).

He described his slave owning as patriarchal: "I do all I can to make [my slaves] comfortable, and they love me like a father. They would do anything on earth to please me. Once I stayed away longer than usual and they thought I was dead. When I reached home they overwhelmed me with their caresses; I could hardly stand it." To a question regarding runaway slaves, he said, "I should be the last man on earth to give up a runaway. If my own were to run away I wouldn't go after 'em" (Child 1970, 157).

Did Kingsley feel no remorse about his slave-trading days? the interviewer wondered. "Some things I do not like to remember," he answered, "but they were not things in which I was to blame; they were inevitably attendant on the trade." And he repeated the idea that had evidently justified his slave-owning life: "To do good in the world you must have money. That's the way I reasoned when I carried on the slave trade. It was very profitable then." His neighbors today, he pointed out, called him an abolitionist. "I tell them they may do so and welcome for it is a pity they shouldn't have one case of amalgamation to point at." Did Kingsley know that men in New England viewed with equal horror slave traders and pirates? Far from taking offense, Kingsley said he was "glad of it" and predicted with satisfaction that they would "look upon a slaveholder just so by and by. Slave trading was very respectable business when I was young. The first merchants in England and America were engaged in it. Some people hide things which they think other people don't like. I never conceal anything" (Child 1970, 156).

The next year, on 13 September 1843, Zephaniah Kingsley died in New York City while visiting his sister Martha McNeill en route to see his family in Haiti. In a Quaker cemetery in

New York he was buried, consistent with the provisions of his will, "without any religious ceremony whatever, and . . . excused from the usual indiscreet formalities and parade of washing, dressing, etc., or exposure in any way, but removed just as [he] died to the common burying ground," a nonconformist to the end (May 1945, 156).

EIGHT

Jessie Ball duPont, Alfred duPont, and Ed Ball

IN 1926, JESSIE BALL DUPONT AND HER husband, Alfred, came to Florida, her brother Ed Ball in tow, and on the St. Johns River at Jacksonville they built Epping Forest, a magnificent estate not far upriver from the Zephaniah Kingsley plantation on Fort George Island. Also nearby lay the site of Fort Caroline, where nearly four hundred years earlier Spanish troops under Menéndez had massacred the French Huguenot colonists. Among Jessie duPont's many philanthropies would be a contribution toward buying land for the Fort Caroline Memorial. In spite of her enormous wealth, or perhaps because of the responsibilities attending it, Jessie believed that "competency in any field . . . resolves into a matter of discipline. We all have an opportunity to practice discipline and get along together in this grand business of living" (Cheek and Draughon 1985, 48). As an acquaintance pointed out, however, Jessie duPont's was a "joyous discipline."

Alfred duPont, one of the wealthy duPonts of Wilmington, Delaware, had visited Florida often since childhood when he and his mother stayed at the Putnam Hotel overlooking the St. Johns at Palatka. He, Jessie, and Ed arrived in Jacksonville soon after the Florida land boom of 1924–25 had fizzled, choosing that city because it was the state's financial center and they intended to minister to Florida's ailing economy. "We don't want any more money and we shall make none for some time," Alfred said then. "But in the long run the things we do . . . will have to pay. Profit is the water that turns the wheels of any sound economy" (James 1941, 400). Alfred duPont described his brother-in-law Ed Ball as "tenacious as a bull dog on a tramp's pants" (James 1941, 360). Known more for his sharp business sense than for his philanthropy, Ed dedicated his adult life to increasing Alfred duPont's estate, a charitable effort in the end, for Jessie Ball and Alfred duPont directed nearly all of their many millions to needy children and the aged and to educational and religious institutions.

In 1884, the year President Grover Cleveland was elected to his first term, Jessie Dew Ball was born on 20 January, a descendant of Mary Ball of Epping Forest, Virginia, the mother of George Washington. (The original Epping Forest, northeast of London, was in colonial times a vast royal hunting ground.) Jessie was born at Hardings, Virginia, a settlement near Cressfield, her father's plantation on a small peninsula called Ball's Neck on the larger peninsula of Northern Neck, where Epping Forest lies. Northern Neck juts out into Chesapeake Bay, bounded by the Potomac River on the north, the Rappahannock on the south. The Balls were numbered among the FFV, the first families of Virginia, which meant that Jessie's ancestors were early Virginia colonists and that the family had continued to be responsible leaders in the country and the community. The designation has little to do with wealth.

Captain Thomas Ball, Jessie's father, had fought under Lee in the Civil War, called by some Ball's Neck residents the War of Northern Aggression. Before returning to his family roots in tidewater Virginia, Ball had served as assistant attorney general of Texas and as a Texas state senator and had briefly practiced law in Baltimore. During Jessie's childhood her father not only ran the Cressfield plantation but practiced law up and down Northern Neck (James 1941, 135).

Ball's Neck lies in the heart of colonial Virginia, only miles from some of America's most historic sites. Up the Potomac is Stratford, the birthplace of Robert E. Lee and his ancestors, signers of the Declaration of Independence. George

Left to right: Isabel Ball, Rebecca Harding and Jessie Ball. Picture taken by Alfred duPont in 1903 at Ball's Neck. From the collection of the Jessie Ball duPont Religious, Charitable, and Educational Fund, Jacksonville.

Washington was born nearby at Wakefield. South from Cressfield is Ditchley, a colonial home built by another Lee and once owned by a Ball relation, and just short of the Rappahannock stands Christ Church, Anglican. Farther south, across the Rappahannock, the ruins of Jamestown overlook the north shore of the James River. Not far away lies Williamsburg, surrounded by colonial plantation homes. Children growing up on Ball's Neck must have breathed in history with their nursery rhymes. "For a backwoods community with few roads," Jessie Ball would say later, "we managed to produce some pretty sound Americans" (Cheek and Draughon 1985, 46).

In the late 1800s, Ball's Neck boasted at least ten plantations, a rural school, a small church, and abundant deer, tur-
key, duck, quail, and fish. On family fishing trips, Jessie often
outfished her two sisters and two brothers. Word of the peninsula's fine hunting and fishing reached north to Wilmington,
Delaware, and brought to Cressfield in 1899, when Jessie Ball
was fifteen and her brother Ed eleven, thirty-five-year-old Alfred duPont.

"No privilege exists which is not inseparably bound to a
duty," went a piece of advice passed down from Huguenot
Pierre Samuel duPont de Nemours to his great-great-grand-
son Alfred Irénée duPont (Carr 1964, 20). Born 12 May
1864, Alfred duPont would eventually combine the visionary
idealism of Pierre duPont de Nemours and the practical genius
of his great-grandfather, Eleuthère Irénée duPont. An econo-
mist and statesman, Pierre duPont de Nemours had been
knighted by Louis XVI and was described by Thomas Jefferson as the most able man in France (James 1941, 16; Carr
1964, 19). Out of the chaos of the French Revolution he
sailed for America with his son in 1799, one step ahead of the
guillotine, intending to establish a large colony on the Ohio
River dedicated to liberty and the pursuit of agriculture and
mechanics, a vision that never materialized (James 1941,
16). His son, Alfred's great-grandfather, Eleuthère Irénée
duPont, soon after arriving in America founded the duPont
gunpowder company near Wilmington. Of Alfred's immediate family, his mother died in a sanitarium, where she had
gone to recover from a nervous breakdown (James 1941,
22), and his father died shortly thereafter, leaving Alfred
at thirteen the eldest male in a family of five children. He
attended MIT, found that producing gunpowder interested
him more than academics, and left college to work in
the family factory. In 1887, at twenty-three, he married
Bessie Gardner, who had been his younger brother Louis's
girlfriend. A few years later, Louis committed suicide during a visit to Alfred and Bessie (Carr 1964, 217, 247). After
twelve years the marriage had produced four children but little harmony, and frequent informal separations had become
routine.

At the Ball's plantation in 1899 and during succeeding hunting seasons, duPont found the warmth and happiness of a large, rural, down-to-earth family (James 1941, 135, 136). He walked the beach with Jessie, occasionally helped her wash dishes, danced with her in the evenings. Ed sometimes went along on the hunting trips, an activity forbidden females, so that Jessie was ordinarily restricted to fishing trips and picnics with the visiting hunters and fishers. "Little Ed Ball" at that time was "a boy who swam through the island swamps and woods like a tadpole, and who could smell a covey of bobtails a mile off, was as sharp as a needle and as mischievous as a puppy" (Mosley 1980, 186).

Ed, like his future brother-in-law Alfred, discovered that academia was not for him. When he was about thirteen he was sent to school in Baltimore, an experience he described some years later to a friend, Fred Schultz. As Schultz recollects, Ed feared that in the big city school his small size would invite violence from larger classmates, so on the first day he carried a half brick with him. When an older boy decided he wanted Ed's lunch, Ed used the brick. Next day, same scenario, this time featuring Ed armed with a brass doorknob. A meeting with the school principal found the two in agreement that Ed and the big city school should part ways, and Ed went back to Ball's Neck and free enterprise. At first he searched out and sold black walnut trees to the Baltimore lumber market by day and protected his father's oyster beds with a shotgun by night. By the time he was fourteen, he was supervising a crew of eighty-five workers in a nearby tomato-canning plant (Mason and Harrison 1976, 9).

Jessie, too, received a practical education, assisting her attorney father who admired her "get up and git." "When I was about thirteen I coaxed him to let me help him, and I would drive through the familiar countryside to pay his bills and collect his legal fees. 'Now Baby,' he used to say as he tucked the lap robe of the old buggy over my knees (and I stuck one of those long hat-pins we used to wear through the thick cloth just in case I might need a little protection), 'you pay my bills and collect my fees and I'll give you a percentage of what you bring back.'" Since teenagers seldom handled hard cash in those days, Jessie viewed her trips as "big business" and later said the experience "developed my horse sense, besides sharpening my wits and teaching me how to deal with people" (Cheek and Draughon 1985, 46, 47). Jessie also helped care for and feed the horses, chickens, and livestock. Besides the usual housekeeping activities shared by females on the plantation, she grew adept at making mechanical and general repairs around the house and on farm equipment. The informal education that would perhaps serve her best, however, was talking with her father about business transactions, investments, and points of law.

Unlike her brother Ed, Jessie took to formal education and in her late teens attended Wytheville Seminary and Farmville Normal School (later Longwood College), both in southwestern Virginia. Her studies complete, at eighteen she was teaching all grades in a country school in Lancaster County. At the end of her first year of teaching, she was awarded a life certificate qualifying her to teach in any Virginia school. The following year she moved to another rural school near Cressfield in Northumberland County before moving to California (*Who Was Who* 1973, 202).

In Wilmington that same year, 1902, when the duPont powder company leadership decided to sell out to outsiders, Alfred engineered a coup by which he and his cousins Pierre and Coleman bought out the firm. Coleman, the largest stockholder, became president and Alfred vice president. The company's production workers liked and admired their new young vice president and superintendent (Carr 1964, 228, 230; Mason and Harrison 1976, 26). When they faced any serious difficulty, the word that went out was "Send for the priest and Mr. Alfred" (James 1941, 118). DuPont's annual hunting trip to Ball's Neck in 1904 marked the beginning of a series of difficult years for him. That year in a hunting accident he lost his left eye. Back home, even before his divorce from Bessie was final in 1906, he was calling on his cousin Alicia Maddox, the wife of his male secretary. Not only was Alfred ungenerous in providing for Bessie and their children; he persuaded her to move out of their home and immediately had it destroyed. Once Mrs. Maddox also was divorced, Alfred married her. Their controversial alliance along with his indifferent treatment of Bessie and his children so distressed some of the duPonts that Coleman finally asked Alfred to leave the company. He refused.

One bright spot during these troubled years came in 1905, when Alfred pushed through a profit-sharing plan for duPont company employees, an innovation he viewed not only as fair but as a way to prevent labor problems. "Surpluses are created to take care of stockholders' interests," he said. "Why not create them to look after the interest of the creative values represented by salaried and wage employees?" (James 1941, 251; see also 242, 478).

In 1908, the Balls moved to California, where the state board of education granted Jessie authority to teach without a college degree, based on recommendations from Virginia schools and her life certificate. She first taught in the San Diego schools, then became vice principal of one of the largest schools at a time when women were rarely tapped for such spots (Jessie Baker Thompson to Charles Bennett, 30 November 1981, in Bennett Files, University of Florida). Out of her modest but increasing income she set up the first of what would grow to more than a hundred college scholarship programs for needy and worthy students. According to a 30 November 1981 letter to the author from her niece Jessie Baker Thompson, Jessie Ball also became in San Diego "the only woman member of an informal group of professional men who met regularly for discussions concerning various subjects" (duPont Biographical File).

With the Balls in California, Alfred duPont missed personal contact with them, but he and Jessie kept up an irregular though lively correspondence. Difficult times continued. By 1911, the forty-seven-year-old duPont was being eased out of production at the company and his marriage to Alicia had gone sour. The new Mrs. duPont had brought her daughter, also named Alicia, with her to the marriage, but both the duPonts' own children had died in infancy. Although they had later adopted Denise, an orphaned child of friends of Mrs. duPont's, by that time Mrs. duPont's health was failing. To comfort her, Alfred built Nemours, a seventy-seven-room estate in Wilmington, and another home on Long Island from which he could steer his unsuccessful New York business ventures. The family remained unhappy despite the new estates. At one low point Alfred wrote to Jessie, "What I really am in need of, and what I have been seeking for the past half century, is a word beginning with 's' and ending with 'y', pronounced by some archeologists 'sym-pa-thy'" (James 1941, 329). By the end of the year, Alfred was the target of company criticism for stressing black powder production in the face of declining sales, and he lost his position among the company's leaders. He went to court against Coleman in 1916 to force him to sell his stock to the company rather than to Pierre. When the court upheld Coleman's position, Alfred lost both his title of vice president and his right to be active in company affairs, although he still owned substantial company stock (James 1941, 322, 422).

A few years later, duPont and his stepdaughter took the train to San Diego to visit the Balls, and Mrs. duPont entrained for Charleston and a relative's debut. On 7 January 1920, Jessie rushed from school to meet the duPonts at the station (James 1941, 329), and the three of them went from there to the hotel where Alfred had reservations. Their plans to visit at luncheon the next day were aborted by a wire that night from Charleston: Alicia duPont had died. Back in Wilmington, Alfred arranged an Episcopalian high church funeral for his wife, surprising those family members who had known neither of his confirmation in the Episcopal church when their infant son died nor of Alfred's practice since then of kneeling in daily prayer. Both Alfred and the family denied the rumor that his wife had died of an overdose of painkiller (James 1941, 329, 330; Mosley 1980, 279).

In March, Jessie Ball and her sister Elsie visited Nemours, where Alfred threw a Ball's Neck reunion. Ten months later, on 22 January 1921, Alfred duPont married Jessie Ball in an Episcopal clergyman's study in Los Angeles, with Ed Ball as best man. DuPont's finances had reached their lowest ebb, and for a time he and Jessie closed Nemours to save money. Nevertheless, both duPonts persuaded Ed to leave an $18,000-a-year furniture business in California for $5,000 a year running duPont's experimental tomato-canning factory in Laurel, Maryland. Even though a year later Ed persuaded Alfred to close down the factory, he stayed on with his new brother-in-law and became his trusted right hand (James 1941, 356; Mosley 1980, 318; Mason and Harrison 1976, 31, 32). Around this time Alfred described Ed as only a fond brother-in-law would have dared: "Being a Ball, he is naturally a gentleman and excuse me from living with anybody less. He is a little pig headed—another Ball feature (also a duPont feature, I being the exception)—so it is necessary to hit him over the head with a club once in a while; but he has a well-balanced cabeza and is a fine, loyal, hard worker, as tenacious as a bull dog on a tramp's pants—all qualities appealing most strongly to me" (James 1941, 360).

In 1922, duPont wrote a paean to his marriage. "After one year with The Brid [bride] I must confess that she is a million times more wonderful than I had hoped. Think of spending one whole year with a girl and never a cross word or having the slightest misunderstanding or receiving anything but constant loving, thoughtful devotion!" (James 1941, 329, 346).

Both duPonts made modest investments in the Florida land boom in the early 1920s. In 1923 Jessie bought two lots in Miami for $33,000, held them for a short time, then sold one for $65,000 and the other for $100,000 (James 1941, 396; Mosley 1980, 338). When the boom collapsed, duPont sent Ed Ball to buy up hundreds of thousands of acres in West Florida. In the early thirties he sent Ball to Tallahassee to persuade legislators to build roads to these inaccessible lands and to extend Florida's highway system throughout the state. In Tallahassee, Ball's base of operations, an old mansion, was dubbed the Highwayman's Hideout (Mosley 1980, 344).

Jessie Ball and Alfred duPont became legal residents of Jacksonville in 1926 and in 1927 moved into Epping Forest, the Spanish-style residence they built on the east bank of the St. Johns. Perhaps the most spectacular house on the river, Epping Forest is smaller than Nemours with its seventy-seven rooms, for Jessie liked to manage her own households when she was in residence and intended to limit the time this task took in Florida (James 1941, 402, 405). She also gardened at all three estates (Nemours, Ditchley, and Epping Forest) and, a legacy from her growing-up years, took on minor household repairs.[1] Alfred was not only mechanically inclined but all his life enjoyed complicated mechanical and inventive projects.

1. Jessie duPont bought Ditchley, near her childhood home and Ball's Neck, as a country retreat. It is still maintained for her relatives' use.

From the flowing well at Epping Forest he created a huge waterwheel to furnish electricity, and a similar project at Nemours on occasion drew Jessie and Ed Ball out in their dinner or evening clothes, where they worked with greasy wrenches into the early hours.[2]

One of his motives for moving to Florida, Alfred duPont said at the time, was to help shore up the state's economy. An early chance came with the financial crash of 1929. "When . . . Florida's banking structure was toppling," *Time* magazine reported on 31 August 1931, "a Strong Man came to save it. He was Alfred Irénée duPont, stormiest of the great Wilmington family. . . . To Florida he brought new sound banks, all with the name Florida National." Alfred relied heavily in this venture on Ed Ball, whose contributions ranged from talking with people standing in line in a run on a bank to standing guard over cash. One night Ball slept at Epping Forest with a sack of money on one side, a shotgun on the other (Mason and Harrison 1976, 49; James 1941, 485), then delivered the money to the Florida National Bank of Jacksonville the next morning. At one time during the depression, Alfred ran a private relief program for Jacksonville's unemployed, paying out of his own pocket the wages of anyone willing to work in the public parks or on other public projects (James 1941, 474).

Alfred duPont did not confine his generosity during the depression to Floridians. When the Delaware legislature failed to pass an old-age pension bill in 1929, duPont set up his own pension system. Nearly a thousand people over sixty-five received payments from him until the state finally acted.

2. As a college student and then as a young lawyer, the author often escorted Denise, the duPonts' adopted daughter, to dances, dinners, and other social events, sometimes at Epping Forest or aboard the duPont yacht, *Nenemoosha*, which usually tied up at the foot of Stonewall Street a few blocks from his family home on Riverside Avenue. Alfred duPont was by then almost entirely deaf, so that Bennett's side of most of the conversations took place on a small pad of paper. "I found him friendly and supportive, never condescending. His wife was a sparkling conversationalist, charming and warm." Other frequent visitors were Ed Ball and his wife, Ruth, and Jessie's sisters, Elise Bowley and Isabel Baker, and their husbands, Major General Albert Bowley and N. Addison Baker. The author's personal observations in the rest of this chapter are included in the hope of adding a dimension to the characters.

Alfred I. duPont and Jessie Ball duPont in 1926 when they became Florida citizens and began the construction of Epping Forest. From the collection of the Jessie Ball duPont Religious, Charitable, and Educational Fund, Jacksonville.

In Jacksonville as in Wilmington, Jessie had an office next to her husband's. "After Mr. duPont and I were married," she once explained, "he . . . encouraged me to cope with business affairs," to take the office next to his and help with his letters, "for he dictated like a whirlwind" (Cheek and Draughon 1985, 46–47). During the business boom of the twenties, Jessie was "buying and selling much more heavily than her conservative husband" (James 1941, 529). Although she lost about $200,000 in the stock market crash, she refused Alfred's offer to bail her out because, as she informed him, she had still come out ahead by over a million dollars (James 1941, 529). She became increasingly important to Alfred's business life, partly because in his deafness he relied upon her to serve as his ears at business meetings. More and more now she "assumed a role of responsibility in the management of her husband's affairs" (James 1941, 529). Roger Main, Jessie's friend and close business associate, said that "her acumen and sound judgment in business affairs constituted an abiding guide and counsel which [Alfred] many times acknowledged" (Gaines 1959, 10). Jessie's concern over how duPont's huge fortune was invested and distributed took its toll, and in January 1930 she was hospitalized with internal bleeding ulcers. Alfred diagnosed the ulcers as the result of overwork, despaired that she might not survive, and wrote a poem, a line of which ran, "Oh Beauty, thou flower of unsurpassed fragrance, how brief is thy lifetime, how fleeting thy breath." When he read it to Jessie after she had recovered, she told him, "You can't get rid of me like a sweet pea. I'm a perennial" (Mosley 1980, 340).

During these years Jessie accomplished a reconciliation between Alfred and his children, and to a large degree the frictions with his more remote relations also dissolved. DuPonts of all ages had come to love and respect Jessie Ball.

Early in 1935, Alfred duPont became convinced that he would soon be "crossing the creek," a family phrase for dying. On 15 January he signed his last testamentary paper with the principal duPont law firm, Knight, Adair, Cooper & Osborne, where this author worked as a law clerk. The question Bennett researched was whether a new Florida law that voided certain types of gifts within the last six months of life would void certain of duPont's desires regarding donations to various charities. On the basis of his brief, the law firm recommended making the desired changes by codicil to preserve the basic thrust of the philanthropic desires expressed in the original will. DuPont suggested to Jessie that the heavy workload required to execute the will would make her a "galley slave," so she might prefer not to be the executrix. Jessie said she felt up to it and was so named, since they both knew that she would understand better than anyone else what Alfred wanted done. Still, the essence of what he wanted done was no secret. When he and Ed had successfully defeated a proposed Florida income tax and a reporter had asked Jessie what she would do with all the money she had thus saved, she answered, "Every cent of it will go to our charity for orphans," and Alfred had chimed in, "And so will the rest of my money" (Mosley 1980, 345).

In March, Alfred had another premonition of his death, and one afternoon he told Elise Bowley to take Jessie on a trip to Europe the next year because he would not be living then to take her himself. That spring, several people close to him noticed that his hands trembled when he worked with heavy tools such as wrenches, but his mind at seventy-seven seemed as sharp as ever. Two weeks before his death, he and Jessie spent a few days on a trip up the St. Johns on their houseboat, the *Gadfly*, and up until days before his death, he was at work in his Jacksonville office. On 29 April 1935, his premonitions proved correct, and Alfred Irénée duPont died at Epping Forest with Jessie at his side (James 1941, 538–42).

The previous year, Alfred wrote a philosophical letter to Dr. Baker Lee, the clergyman who had married Jessie and him in 1921:

> My philosophy of life is exceedingly simple: be fair to everyone; do as much good as you can; be honest with yourself, which means, honest with everybody; and to put it mildly, be most disagreeable to anyone who seeks to do you injury. . . . As for my philosophy for the future, it is equally simple. One's proper discharge of one's duties and obligations in this world will insure proper recognition in the next—about which, of course, I know nothing. . . . That there must be a Divine Providence, as Creator of the Universe, one can hardly deny. Of this fact

even a small lightning bug that alighted on my hand the other evening in the loggia at Nemours, would convince one. . . . It is impossible to conceive a future life of happiness without those with whom we have lived in this world—Mummy [his dog] included! (James 1941, 531)

Although Alfred's will did not require his major philanthropies to be in place until after Jessie's death, she and her brother Ed immediately began allocating the funds. To fulfill Alfred's desire to provide employment for West Florida citizens, they set up in 1935 the St. Joe Paper Company at Port St. Joe; it would become one of the largest such firms in the country (Griffith 1975, 108; Gaines 1959, 16; James 1941, 532–36). They also acquired for the estate the bankrupt Florida East Coast Railroad (Bank Files; Florida East Coast Railroad Files; Mason and Harrison 1976, 58, 67, 79–86; *Florida Suntime* 1953, 8). In 1936, Jessie chartered the Nemours Foundation to oversee the planning and operation of the Alfred I. duPont Institute for treating crippled children.

The principal responsibility for handling Alfred's vast estate lay with Jessie. In a letter to the author dated 3 August 1983, her friend and employee Hazel Williams (later executive secretary of the Jessie Ball duPont Religious, Charitable and Educational Fund) wrote that she had seen Mrs. duPont "stand up to Mr. Ball and other executive officers and staff of the various interests owned by Mr. duPont's Estate, when she disagreed with some of the proposals or investments. Some of the newcomers to these organizations, and some not so new, soon became aware, after being skeptical of a woman in such a position of authority, of her wise judgment, and especially appreciated her warmth and understanding of their business problems and her genuine interest in their families" (duPont Biographical File). In 1941, Jessie dedicated the Alfred I. duPont Institute, which opened on the grounds of Nemours. According to Hazel Williams, "she was very, very proud of the Institute and would tell stories of some of the boys and girls who might enter the Institute 'on all fours' and then later, after treatment, walk out, maybe wearing braces, but proud and erect" (duPont Biographical File).

After Alfred's death Mrs. duPont not only assumed heavy financial responsibilities but also began supervising the maintenance crew on the estates, in addition to the household staff. Hazel Williams wrote that "she could speak with authority and understanding on painting, plumbing, electrical work, dock and boat maintenance, carpentry and other matters, normally left up to the men in the family. She loved blueprints and would spend a great deal of time conferring with her workmen and with organizations she supported when they would bring their plans around regarding new construction and renovation, even though in most instances they did not expect her to contribute toward the cost, knowing her feeling about 'giving to buildings'" (J. B. duPont File, Gainesville). She preferred to donate directly and usually anonymously to individuals, for she believed that otherwise the needs of people often were overlooked by those intent on building monuments to the givers.

During World War II, Hazel Williams remembers, Jessie wrote to a number of servicemen overseas and insisted on making the same wartime sacrifices as other citizens and using only the legal gas ration. Each day she drove as far as her rationed gas would allow, then walked (or in bad weather rode the streetcar) the additional mile or two to the office (duPont Biographical File). During the war years the U.S. Military Chaplains Association gave Jessie its award for "distinguished service to God and Country," mainly for "her patronage of the work of all chaplains" (Cheek and Draughon 1985, 44). From the hands of England's George VI came a special medal recognizing Jessie's leadership in the British War Relief Society (Bundles for Britain), and on the invitation of Elizabeth II she was made a member of the Order of the Hospital of St. John and received the civilian form of the St. George Cross.

Jessie Thompson, Jessie duPont's niece, in a letter of 30 November 1981 to the author, recalled a wartime visit to Epping Forest: "With gas rationing there were not as many visitors back and forth as she usually had so we looked at books in the evenings . . . particularly art books as I had finished Wellesley, majoring in art history, not long before. My Aunt could outstrip me every time in naming the artist, title, and the place of the work of art—whether painting, sculpture, or architecture. It was obvious that she had a great love of these and remembered them from her travels" (duPont Biographical File).

Jessie's recreation more often tended toward the vigorous—gardening, fishing, and boating. A favorite activity was fishing for sea bass with William C. Munds, at one time rector of Christ Church, Episcopal, in Wilmington, and Mrs. Munds on visits to their home in Cuttyhunk, Massachusetts. On nights with a full moon, the fishing party set out around midnight in an open boat, often in rough seas. One season Jessie won a medal for the prize catch and had the fish stuffed and hung at the duPont Institute at Nemours. Hazel Williams recalled in a letter of 3 August 1983 to the author that when Mrs. duPont first saw the bass on the wall she said, "My fish either shrunk or they swapped fishes on me" (duPont Biographical File).

In 1951, Governor Fuller Warren appointed Jessie duPont to the Florida's Board of Control, which supervised the state universities. She was then sixty-seven years old. Warren was quoted in a 17 September news release as saying that Mrs. duPont, the board's first woman member, had "attained her highest fame in the field of finance and business" (duPont Biographical File). Eli Fink, a Jacksonville attorney and fellow board member, wrote about Jessie's contributions to the board in a letter to the author dated 9 February 1984. From the perspective of some forty years, he wrote:

All of us men then serving on the Board were somewhat apprehensive as to what effect a woman on the Board would have on our meetings, many of which lasted long after midnight and sometimes were the occasions for comments which in those days were not usually made in the presence of ladies. All of us were completely delighted with our new member. Mrs. duPont possessed an extraordinary combination of charm, business acumen, wit and dignity, which gently but firmly demanded and received attention and respect. . . .

Mrs. duPont . . . [had a] remarkable ability to analyze and evaluate factors involved in business and financial matters. This was demonstrated at our Board meetings time and again by her views on many of the financial matters which required our attention and especially those involved in the operations of the University of Florida, Florida State University and Florida A. and M. (duPont Biographical File)

In a 17 February 1984 letter to the author, the board's corporate secretary during Jessie's tenure, Dr. J. Broward Culpepper, echoed Fink's praise and added that "Mrs. duPont made many contributions to worthy and needy students, to programs requiring financial assistance and to research which otherwise would not have been activated. Furthermore through her persuasion and interest Board members and Cabinet members frequently brought benefits to the University System which otherwise might not have taken place" (duPont Biographical File).

Jessie duPont was also the first woman trustee of Washington and Lee University in its two-hundred-year history. (In a letter to the author dated 27 September 1980, Ed Ball wrote that Jessie "would not accept the many invitations to go on various boards unless she was sure she would be able to be an active board member. She felt that one should not merely lend her name, but become a part of the discussions and decisions" [Ball File].) The author often talked with her about her keen interest in independent colleges, and in a rare interview published in the *Tampa Sunday Tribune* on 26 June 1955, she said that "with full appreciation of the role played by our state institutions," independent institutions of higher learning would die without corporate contributions. "Industry depends to a great extent on our private institutions for top executives," she pointed out. "Therefore, industry should support these schools. Once we permit our independent colleges to die, the state can take over and dictate education." She warned that such a situation exists in communist countries, and "We do not want that to happen in this land."

She worried about the quality of education children received in the public schools and about the dull textbooks they read. Our grade schools, she thought, failed "to stimulate a child's mind, to hold his interest." In the past, by the sixth grade a student had acquired "some of the greatest literary and poetic gems, as well as knowledge of our patriotic incidents and heroes of this country and the world. Text books in our grade schools today lack stimulating material of this kind." How can our universities, she asked, "build a superstructure on the faulty foundation turned out of the public schools?" (*Tampa Sunday Tribune*, 26 June 1955). She also favored the congressional legislation the author introduced in 1963 to encourage the teaching of ethical standards in public schools. "Why shouldn't we teach the Ten Commandments?" she wanted to know. "After all, the Commandments are the law on which our country stands" (duPont Biographical File).

But Jessie duPont's strongest ties with education came through her scholarships for deserving college students, a program that had its beginnings out of her assistant principal's salary in San Diego and eventually ballooned to help 150 students each year. Jessie Thompson wrote to the author on 30 November 1981 that her aunt awarded the scholarships only "after looking carefully into the personal need; and regular and satisfactory progress reports were required for the scholarship to be continued. Some of her scholars went on to great success in life, came to know her well, and wished to repay her" (duPont Biographical File). One of these students, Thomas Rice, visited Jessie duPont in Wilmington after he graduated.

She promptly responded that she did not want the money back, but she wanted me to do the same for someone else and to let her know when this happened. Accordingly it was my good fortune to be able to fulfill this commitment and to let Mrs. duPont know that it had been done.

Her generosity to me as an individual has been so meaningful during my entire adult life, and made possible a future in the business world that has been both interesting and fulfilling. The greatest honor that has come to me, however, through the years was a handwritten congratulatory letter from Mrs. duPont telling me that "you are the best investment I ever made." For this and many memorable visits and discussions I shall always revere her memory. (Cheek and Draughon 1985, 15)

According to a letter Ed Ball wrote the author on 27 September 1980, the individual scholarship program finally grew too large for Jessie and her secretary to manage, and she started making contributions to schools and colleges for scholarship purposes (Ball File).

In 1966, Florida East Coast Railroad employees went on strike, and the unions asked for an amendment of the federal law exempting labor unions, agriculture organizations, and philanthropic testamentary trusts from bank holding company restrictions. The restrictions applied to companies that owned banks as well as some other business, the best interests of which might conflict with the bank's. The unions wanted the

Ed Ball at age seventy-five. From the Jessie Ball duPont Religious, Charitable, and Educational Fund, Jacksonville.

amendment to eliminate the exemption for trusts, so that the duPont trust (and Ed Ball) would have to give up the railroad. The author at that time represented Jacksonville in Congress, and Mr. Ball explained to him that he objected not to eliminating the exceptions but to singling out only the exception for trusts. Although the House removed all the exceptions, the Senate eliminated only testamentary trusts, and that was how the law finally passed in 1966. In 1978, the remaining exceptions were eliminated for the future. Nevertheless the unions failed to achieve their end. Jessie and Ed decided to give up control of the banks rather than control of the railroad. The unions continued the strike.

On Ed's seventy-fifth birthday, in 1963, the author invited him to be his guest at breakfast at the Carlton Hotel in Washington. The Jacksonville business community and some labor people had asked him to try to settle the railroad strike, and he intended to try over one of Ed's favorite dishes, thin pancakes softened up with a pitcher of hot honey and melted butter. Bennett suggested that Ed honor Alfred's ideals by offering the labor unions some sort of profit-sharing contract, since the company could not then raise salaries but might be able to do so in a year. He agreed that Bennett might take this up with the union leadership, who proved unwilling to negotiate on that issue. Ed Ball continued to run the trains without the unions, and after years of insolvency the railroad became a financial success.

Jessie continued to spend most of her energy on deciding how to allocate the duPont fortune. She once told the author that she felt responsible for seeing that "each dollar went thoughtfully to a charitable purpose worthy of the expenditure" and that this work often consumed her entire business day. A letter from Ed Ball on 27 September 1980 briefly described her daily program: "You are right about my sister putting in a full day at the office, both in Jacksonville and in Wilmington. Before coming into the office, she would meet with her staff and plan for the day; then go over the grounds with the maintenance men at either 'Epping Forest' or 'Nemours'. She would arrive at the office between ten and eleven o'clock, sometimes earlier, and seldom left before five, never leaving the office for lunch" (Ball File).

Ed went on to tell how Jessie dealt with requests for donations: "No letter requesting assistance went unanswered. Many times, somewhat following Mr. duPont's practice, Mrs. duPont would pencil in an amount on the margin of a letter, and turn it over to her secretary for handling. Requests from small Churches received the same treatment" (Ball File). Jessie did give anonymously to many churches. She, the author, and Bishop Frank Juhan, Episcopal bishop of Florida, once talked about the needs of churches, and the bishop mentioned that Mrs. duPont had funded the brick walk at Falls Church in Virginia. He said that building the walk today cost more than building the first church had cost Augustine Washington in 1734 and more than the 1767 structure still in use today built by Augustine's son, George. Mrs. duPont also helped preserve and maintain Christ Church, Anglican, near her childhood home in Virginia. In another incident involving men of the cloth, at a Wilmington tea party the Episcopal bishop drank a scotch with Jessie when other clergymen present chose not to imbibe. The next day, so the story goes, the bishop's diocese received a large donation (Reese 1977, 62–64).

Not all the requests for donations came with the credibility of the clergy behind them, Ed Ball recollected in his 1980 letter. "It worried Mrs. duPont that it soon became evident that she could not take letters at face value, that some investigation needed to be made. Someone told me of an instance where a request came in asking her to purchase a new Chevrolet car for her so that she could take her children to their various activities and take her little crippled child for rides. Mrs. duPont responded that though she couldn't purchase a new car for her, she would like to know more about the 'little crippled child'." Ed wrote that Jessie liked to contribute to "fine, hardworking people who because of serious illness or other misfortune, found themselves in a situation where just a little 'long green' might put them back on their feet." He cited "her gifts at Christmas and Easter to the residents in two Wilmington nursing homes. She would purchase cards and place a twenty dollar bill in each—almost one hundred guests in each home—and send them for distribution to these ladies, 'for a trip to the five and dime, or ye olde beauty shoppe'" (Ball File).

When the author was soliciting $40,000 for the first land for the Fort Caroline National Memorial, Jessie gave $10,000. She suggested that soliciting generous gifts is seldom effective unless the solicitor also gives generously, and how large a donation did he intend to make? As it turned out, Bennett contributed almost the entire balance (partly with an interest-free $5,000 loan from financier Bernard Baruch), not such a great burden for the bachelor he then was. Jessie offered to increase her donation when she found out.

Some years later, after Mr. Baruch had died, Fort Caroline needed a sixteenth-century astrolabe and the author asked Ed Ball to succeed him as his interest-free banker. He laughed, said he could lend it at the prime rate (at that time about 4 percent), and, when Bennett repaid him, made a $2,000 gift to the $10,000 project, wiping out the interest and then some. His talk about interest, he said, was meant to see if Bennett was serious. Later Ball told him that he had driven out to see the ancient navigational instrument and thought it a "great purchase." (At the time no other sixteenth-century astrolabe in the world was privately owned as far as could be determined, and the author believes that still to be true.)

Often over the years Jessie had expressed the idea to close friends that she found it "very difficult in this 'man's world' for a woman with the responsibilities which I have inherited" (Hazel Williams to Bennett, 3 August 1983, Bennett Files, University of Florida). When she was seventy-six, Jessie wrote with some wistfulness to her friend Mrs. Alfred (Polly) Shands on 25 April 1960, "I have heard about people being their own bosses,—I'd like to meet one. To go back to my original statement when I was seventeen, I reckon,—'The only fellow who was his own boss was the gentleman of the road, who slept under the haystack, or the rose hedges, with the starry heavens for a canopy.' I think that's about true" (J. B. duPont File, Jacksonville).

As each year of declining health kept Jessie longer at Nemours with its adjacent hospital, she often invited the author and his family to come for a visit; finally they went in the fall of 1970. When they arrived she was so ill the doctors would allow no visitors, and on 26 September she died.

Years later, her brother Ed Ball replied to a birthday greeting the author sent him: "Faith to tell, I like having birthdays because as long as I am having them I am on this side 'of the creek'; and frankly, even though I am an optimist I am uncertain as to what I will find on the other side . . . and I am in no hurry to start exploring" (Ball File). When Bennett visited him in Jacksonville a time or two as he lay in bed at his last home on St. Johns Avenue overlooking the St. Johns River, he found Ball alert and cheerful, although he said that this time his illness was serious and said he would "be going over the creek soon." On 24 June 1981, in Oschner's Clinic in New Orleans, Ed Ball at the age of ninety-three finally joined Jessie Ball and Alfred duPont on the other side of the creek.

NINE

Eartha Mary Magdalene White

TOWARD THE END OF THE 1800S, ABOUT fifty years after Anna Jai Kingsley left Florida for her husband's free black colony in Haiti, Eartha Mary Magdalene White spent part of her childhood in Anna's tabby house on Fort George Island at the mouth of the St. Johns River. Raised by a former slave, the young black girl would try to live by the words her adoptive mother taught her: "Do all the good you can, in all the ways you can, in all the places you can, for all the people you can, while you can." Eartha White's lifetime spanned almost a century, and over the years she would become "a kind of universal mother to much of Jacksonville."[1]

Eartha White was born on 8 November 1876 to Mollie Chapman, a young black woman, and a young man from a prominent white family whose identity White chose not to make public (Schafer 1976, 7; Schafer 1980, 726).[2] Clara White, apparently fulfilling a promise to the natural parents, adopted

1. The author knew Eartha White for most of his life and counts himself among those she mothered. She had confidence that he would do the right thing at all times, that he could do, with God's help, anything he set his mind to do, and that he would not waste his life on trifling or ignoble things.

2. A notation among Eartha's writings identifies the name of the person she apparently believed to be her natural father, but since the identification may be in error and publishing it may unfairly and even inaccurately intrude on the privacy of living persons, that information is not included here.

Eartha soon after her birth and inspired her for the rest of her life. Not long after Clara adopted Eartha, she gave up for adoption her own child of about the same age, Bertha White, and in 1881 her husband, Lafayette White, died, leaving Eartha and Clara a close-knit family of two.

For years Eartha believed that Clara was her natural mother, and the story Clara told the young Eartha about her naming instilled the belief that she was a special person, chosen by God. When she was pregnant with Eartha, Clara told her, she was visited by her cousin, Reverend Henry Harrison, and her father, Adam English. Harrison urged her to name the child Eartha because, he said, "Everything you get comes from the earth. I want her named Eartha so, like God's good earth, she will be a storehouse for all people." Adam English insisted that Clara name the baby Mary Magdalene because that biblical woman had done so much good. According to Clara's story, she promised that if the baby was a girl she would name her Eartha Mary Magdalene.

Similarly, Eartha treasured the story of Clara White's life as a part of her own life pattern, an upward spiral. Clara was born a slave on the Robert Harrison plantation on Amelia Island on 4 July 1845, the year Florida became a state. Clara and her parents were given to Mrs. Harrison as gifts for her "maintenance and support" (Schafer 1976, 3). When Clara was small, she saw her mother, Jane Drummond English, sold away from the family in a slave auction at the northeast corner of Ocean and Forsyth streets in Jacksonville. The selling price of a $1,000 was high, reflecting her proven ability to produce children. Clara would not see her mother again until after the Civil War (Schafer 1976, 3). Mrs. Harrison gave young Clara as a birthday gift to her nephew, Colonel Charles Cooper, Sr. (Schafer 1976, 3), whose children Clara cared for until she was freed by the war. Shortly afterwards, she married Lafayette White, who had served with her father in Company D of the 34th Regiment of U.S. Colored Troops. None of the Whites' twelve children lived to adulthood, with the possible exception of Bertha, who was removed to a northern city in early childhood and of whom no later record could be found. Lafayette became a drayman, while Clara worked as a domestic with several white families, among them possibly the Coopers, her former owners, who continued to help her until she died (Schafer 1976, 5).

During Eartha's early life she and Clara lived on Clay Street in downtown Jacksonville. In her eighties, Eartha recalled those days for a *Florida Times-Union* interviewer in 1958: "We lived in a two-room house over on Clay Street and at Christmas our little fireplace was hung with stockings—oh so many stockings! All of the children came to my mother for Christmas. She bought things—little things, nothing was so elaborate as it is now. She made things. People knew what she was doing and they gave her things for the children. And they all believed, we all believed, that Santa had come and left those things. We never knew it was my mother who gave us these little things. I can see it now."

When Clara went to work for the John Rollins family, who owned the old Kingsley Plantation on Fort George Island, she and Eartha lived in Anna Jai Kingsley's former home (Schafer 1976, 11). For a time Clara worked as a maid in the St. James and Windsor hotels, as a stewardess on steamships on the St. Johns River, and later as a stewardess on the Clyde Line ships that traveled between Florida and New York and New England.

In Jacksonville, Eartha went to Stanton School and the Divinity School (then Cookman Institute, later Bethune-Cookman College). When she was sixteen, in 1893, Jacksonville was put under a yellow fever quarantine, and Clara sent her to New York to stay with Mr. and Mrs. William Gross. There Eartha went to several schools, including Madame Thurber's National Conservatory of Music, where her teacher was a well-known black singer, Harry T. Burleigh. As a result, Eartha joined the Oriental American Opera Company, the country's first black opera company, under the musical direction of J. Rosamond Johnson. (Also a Jacksonville native, Johnson was the brother of writer James Weldon Johnson, composer of the song that became known as the Negro national anthem, "Lift Every Voice and Sing.") The opera company, according to a paper Eartha wrote, was financed by a Syracuse philanthropist "who wanted to prove that Negroes could sing opera music as well as folk songs" (White Collection).

Oriental-American Opera Company, New York City. Earth White is the second woman from the left in the front row. From the Eartha White Collection, University of North Florida Library, Jacksonville.

On occasional trips home to Jacksonville, Eartha fell in love with James Jordan, a young railroad employee, and their wedding was set for June 1896. But Jordan's letters told of increasing illness, and on 3 March he wrote, "Eartha dear, you don't want my photo now. I have lost 16 pounds. . . . I really can hardly keep up some days" (Schafer 1976, 15). While Eartha was on tour in May, news reached her of Jordan's death. It would prove a turning point in her life.

Eartha abandoned her singing career and returned to Jacksonville, vowing to serve mankind. As she later said, she was thereafter "married to the cause of Christ and his kingdom—building for God and humanity." She enrolled at the Florida Baptist Academy in Jacksonville, graduated in 1897, and before the year was out managed a benefit to finance a fence for the county cemetery. During the Spanish-American War in the spring of 1898, she volunteered and nursed the sick and wounded in the armed camp the war made of Jacksonville.

In 1899, Eartha became a public school teacher in Bayard, in the environs of Jacksonville, moonlighting with the Afro American Insurance Company, which led her in 1900 to Boston for the first meeting of the National Negro Business League. There she came to know Booker T. Washington, one of the league's founders. In Jacksonville's great fire of 1901, Eartha saved the insurance company's records by commandeering a dray to rush the files out of harm's way and into the suburbs. The next year she transferred to downtown Jacksonville to teach in Stanton School.

Over the years Eartha began buying real estate at low prices to sell at a profit, and by 1905 she had saved enough to open a dry goods store. In a *New York Times* interview on 4 December 1970, she laughed at her youthful ignorance and grandiose ideas of what her meager cash on hand would buy: "I thought I could buy the world with that $150 but when my merchandise came it was but one crate; and when I complained to the man who sold me the goods that they hadn't come he laughed and said I was sitting on it." She said that at that time she would go down to the docks on the river to get vegetables cheap enough for her poor customers at her Florida Avenue store. In 1912 she helped bring her friend Booker T. Washington to a meeting of the Business League in Jacksonville, and she was subsequently elected official historian of the organization. Eartha sold her store in 1913 for $10,000. In time she established a janitorial contracting service for office buildings, an employment bureau, and a steam laundry, and she went on to become a licensed real estate broker.

After the 1901 fire Clara White and Eartha saw the need for an old people's home in Jacksonville and revived the Union Benevolent Association, which had been founded in 1885 to build such a home. It was the first piece in the Whites' pattern of helping the needy—alcoholics, unwed mothers, tubercular patients, servicemen away from home, the aged, the orphaned, the sick, the handicapped, and the unemployed. Eartha was elected president of the association, and in 1902 she and Clara began to solicit funds. The Old Folks Home became a reality that year, and for many years afterward Eartha remained its chief provider of funds, soliciting money, food, clothing, and medical services from all who would give. She kept the aged in food, clothing, and good health. In those days city councilmen simply referred welfare cases to her.

Eartha's concern spanned the generations. To fight juvenile delinquency she set up the Boys' Improvement Club and in 1906 established a recreational park for youngsters, paying the salary of its management from her own funds for ten years until the city assumed the costs. She successfully lobbied the state legislature for an institution for delinquent girls; after Forest Hills was built near Ocala she often visited there, and one cottage is named for her. On one occasion, according to a report in the 10 August 1957 *Jacksonville Journal*, she assured the girls of her belief that "your coming here was God's way of using you for some purpose. Surely you will not come to an institution like this without leaving a better person. Everyone can do something for God. You have to decide what your place is in life and get into it."

Around the same time Eartha began visiting prisoners in the county stockade every Sunday and conducting Sunday school there, a practice she would continue for the next fifty years. She took little gifts and Scripture verses. Every week she went by the King Edward cigar factory to pick up cigars "for the boys in prison." A *Jacksonville Journal* article on 7 July 1933 reported that through twenty-five years of visits the prisoners had come to look on her as "mother, sister and benefactor."

At least one man looked on Eartha White with a more intimate eye. Albert C. Sammis, a railroad employee who lived at Port Tampa, not only wrote Eartha love letters but wooed her through letters to her mother. "Eartha can have anything she wants and me too whenever she gets ready," he wrote Clara, then urged her to persuade Eartha to come to Tampa for a fair. "Tell her to come and spend that time with me and I will make it pleasant for her. I will have a lady in the house so she won't be alone with an old bachelor. Let her come, mother dear. You can trust her with me."

During World War I, Eartha was War Camp Community Services director and recreation coordinator for servicemen in Savannah. She was the only black to attend President Wilson's Council on National Defense at the White House.

At the time of what would prove to be Clara White's final

illness, Albert wrote Eartha, "Please remember, my love, that Albert and everything that's Alberts is yours. Oh how I wish you could learn to feel and think that way of me. Remember no matter what happens you are not alone. You will have one who will die for you if necessary." Clara died on 20 July 1920, when Eartha was forty-four. She went on to expand the settlement work begun by Clara on First Street, then moved to a better site at 611 Ashley Street, where the Clara White Mission still operates. Among the letters that Eartha saved, along with Albert Sammis's love letters, was one dated 17 November 1921 that read, "I am thankful for my socks and shoes and dress because I didn't have a stocking to my feets. I am thankful you are helping unable people. May God bless you."

But Eartha White was as politically astute as she may have been sentimental. On 6 November 1920, the Duval County Republican party passed a resolution thanking Eartha M. M. White, "the energetic faithful committee representative, leader of the Colored Women Republican Voters," for her hard work, excellent results, and the able leadership that made her "the right woman leader in the right place" (White Collection).[3] Partly because the southern Democrats did not welcome blacks into their ranks until after World War II, by the 1928 election campaigns Eartha was state chairwoman of the National League of Republican Colored Women, working with enthusiasm and effect to elect Herbert Hoover over Al Smith. On 23 November 1928, the Republican National Committee wrote her, "We have indeed won a tremendous victory, and under the sound business leadership of Mr. Hoover will understandably show marked progress during the next decade."

At the same time she was expanding Clara White's settlement work, Eartha in the twenties continued to minister to children. Although the Children's Home Society was begin-

3. Unless otherwise noted, the Eartha White Collection contains all source material for the remainder of this chapter. The author is especially indebted to Daniel L. Schafer of the Department of History at the University of North Florida for information found in his typescript "Eartha White: The Early Years of a Jacksonville Humanitarian," located in the White Collection in the University of North Florida Library.

Eartha White at dedication of her nursing home in Jacksonville in 1967.

ning to place children for adoption throughout most of the state, in 1921 Marcus Fagg, its superintendent, had to reply to a request from Jasper, Florida, "Our society does not handle any colored children at all, and you might be able to secure such a child by writing Eartha White, colored, Eagle Street, Jacksonville, who conducts some sort of an orphanage or children's home." Eartha also maintained a place on Minor Street for all children she could not place in private homes.

Albert Sammis's love letters continued to arrive. "You are the most wonderful girl in the world," he wrote Eartha, now fifty-three, on 31 January 1929. "You do what no one else could." It was a good thing she did, because through the doors of the Clara White Mission over the next few years came a wave of the depression's unemployed, and to each went a meal of soup or a basket of groceries or some shoes or clothing. In one of her pleas for support for the mission, Eartha pointed out that tragedy was no respecter of economics: "There are no slump periods in this business of relief, for the sick, the halt, and the poor we have always with us. For them the rise and fall of the stock market has no significance; they are neither enriched nor further impoverished by any change in the governing parties. The stock ticker that records their destinies is the pulsation of the Human Heart, and the party of their salvation is the party in whose heart Charity dwells."

Eartha White was in her sixties when World War II brought new opportunities for service. The mission added a program for area armed forces personnel, and Eartha became an honorary colonel of the Women's National Defense Program under honorary general Mary McLeod Bethune and coordinated canteen and Red Cross activities for all service people in Florida. She also helped plan Jacksonville's participation in the war camp effort as the only woman on a sixty-member interracial War Camp Community Service Conference.

Although Eartha seldom talked about purely racial issues, she observed that "much too much importance is given to the color of the skin in this world of ours" and that "when God made man He made him out of the earth, neither black nor white, and man's true color is the color of the earth." Among her intimate friends were A. Philip Randolph, another Jacksonville native, and Mary McLeod Bethune, whom Eartha occasionally visited at Bethune-Cookman College in Daytona. Unlike the approach taken by many of other black leaders Eartha's was benevolent, her message a quiet one: "Blacks want to be treated as Christian brothers and sisters, not as exotics." Her friend Charles Brooks, principal of Stanton High School, once pointed out that the Confederate flag on the Congressman Bennett's wall in Washington would offend some constituents. He advised Bennett to weigh each issue according to what was right, not what was easy or expedient. When Eartha White came to Washington to support some legislation, Bennett asked her to lunch in the House restaurant. "Thank you," she said, a question in her eyes, "but I have already eaten." On being told what Charles Brooks had said to Bennett, she was asked to eat a ceremonial bowl of soup. Her eyes twinkled, then she laughed outright. "Yes," she said, "I really want to go—I've heard about the marvelous bean soup they serve there." And the lunch took place.

On 10 September 1955, when Eartha returned from a trip to Europe paid for by friends who had decided she needed a rest, the *Jacksonville Journal* dubbed her "Angel of Mercy." For an angel, she was receiving a host of worldly awards and honors—among them the Good Citizenship Award from the Jacksonville Jaycees, the Booker T. Washington Symbol of Service Award from the National Business League, and several honorary degrees including a Doctor of Laws from Edward Waters College. She helped found the National Association of Colored Women and belonged to the National Council of Negro Women.

A moment of special joy came during Eartha's eighty-ninth year on 19 December 1965 with the groundbreaking for the 122-bed Eartha M. M. White Nursing Home on Moncrief Road. The $780,000 nursing home was built in part with a federal grant, announced on the floor of the House on 3 February 1965. In a letter of thanks dated 1 February, Eartha wrote the author that "since service is the price you pay for the space you occupy, undoubtedly the size of your space is beyond imagination" (Bennett Files). The home was dedicated and opened for use on 5 March 1967. Later that year, Eartha's ninety-first, she wrote the author for help to get funds for on-the-job training programs for the disadvantaged. By that time Eartha's birthday parties were being held in Jacksonville's civic auditorium, and at one of them, after the author had voted against the 1964 civil rights bill, Eartha introduced him as "a friend," adding, "and you know what a friend is; it's someone you know all about but you still love."

On 3 December 1970, at a ceremony in New York City, Eartha White received the 1970 Lane Bryant Award for "the person in America considered to have made the most outstanding voluntary contribution to his or her community during the past year" (Bennett Files). She was ninety-four years old. Following the ceremony, Eartha was President Nixon's honor guest at a White House reception, and before the year was out she was back at the White House for a conference on aging. The following year, on 27 April 1971, she received a

Eartha White at age ninety-four, three years before her death. Photo by Ricardo Ferro, from the *Floridian* news magazine, Tampa, 1 August 1971.

standing ovation when she took her seat on the National Center for Volunteer Action board of directors to which President Nixon had appointed her. Also in 1971 Florida's Governor Reubin Askew presented Eartha a certificate naming her as the state's outstanding senior citizen, and the American Nursing Home Association gave her its highest award.

On 18 January 1974, Eartha Mary Magdalene White died at age ninety-seven.[4] She was buried in the old city cemetery in Jacksonville. A feature article in the 1 August 1971 *Floridian* described her greatness in simple terms: "She is, quite simply, an institution in Jacksonville. Each November 8 her birthday is celebrated in the city's civic auditorium. There are brick and wood and stone buildings that are her work. A dirt street bears her name. But more importantly Eartha M. M. White represents a mélange of memories and envy and admiration of White and Black minds. She is a kind of universal mother to much of Jacksonville, particularly to the ghetto. She is the good earth."

4. The rumor that Eartha was wealthy had no basis in fact. She left nearly all she possessed to charities—less than $50,000, including some real estate.

Afterword

TO RECORD HISTORY PROPERLY, IT MUST
be done objectively. Yet a strong reason for this book was the
inspirational qualities of the lives of the people discussed, and
telling of inspiration objectively is like describing good food
without smelling or tasting it. So the publisher was prevailed
upon to allow the author the following subjective comments.

Jean Ribault, a real hero, lived a successful life as a naviga-
tor and a diplomat until his execution at Matanzas. His life was
dedicated to his view of God, Christianity, and religious freedom. Since others with him in 1565 were allowed to recant
their religious beliefs to save their lives, he and Barré probably could have done the same. Instead, they remained true to
principle and paid the price—their lives. In this, they were
truly heroic.

Saturiba, a contemporary of Ribault and Barré, is revealed
by all accounts as a strong, skillful, yet tragic leader, confronted as he was by an overwhelming horde of powerfully
armed strangers from an unknown land. This Indian chief's responsibility to protect his people against adverse and unequal
odds required not just cleverness but brave and decisive leadership. He provided it in abundance.

When Saturiba had to decide where to place his loyalties,

149

he chose his first friends, the French intruders—this despite their manifest imperfections. Could it be that when he insisted that the Ninety-first Psalm be recited by the French in 1567 he sought the words not only as a token of alliance but as an assurance of divine blessing? "My God in him will I trust. He will cover thee with his feathers and under his wing shalt thou trust. A thousand shall fall at thy side and ten thousand at thy right hand; but it shall not come nigh thee. He shall give his angels charge over thee to keep thee in all thy ways."

Father Francisco Pareja's saintliness embraced not only his tremendous spiritual impact upon the Indians but also his personal qualities of humility, sacrifice, and compassion. But there was an activist and controversial side to this spiritual leadership. His actions, correspondence, and conversation with temporal as well as church authorities were direct, forceful, and compelling. He lived a life of passionate Christianity and was considered saintly by his contemporaries. He was seen as a man who had brought about a miracle when his prayer for the survival of a threatened ship in an angry sea was answered. By his candid and courageous arguments with the Spanish king, he achieved most of the objectives he sought for improving missionary work. No one in American history would seem more clearly entitled to the status of sainthood; in fact the Catholic Church is now considering the possibility of bestowing it on Father Francisco Pareja. He appears to deserve it.

Edmund Gray stands out as a fascinating character among fascinating contemporaries. As a legislator in Savannah, he sponsored a bill to lessen property ownership requirements for the voting franchise in order to open greater opportunities for the common man; at New Hanover he achieved one of America's earliest environmental laws—prohibiting the cutting of certain trees. He greatly disturbed the colonial leadership in both Georgia and England. But his controversial actions on the southern frontier may have helped England to acquire Florida: he helped convince the Spanish authorities that Florida's northern borders could not be made secure as long as frontiersmen like him remained in the borderlands under the English flag. In any event, his independence, courage, dedication to the thrust of democracy to include ordinary people must be listed as positive qualities worthy of remembrance today.

Billy Bartram blessed and charmed away all danger from wild animals and Indians on the warpath as he pursued his solitary journeys through the wilderness. In turn, he was blessed by the forces of nature and protected by the natives. At the center of his beliefs was the concept that God exists in all living things. There was a universal love and harmony about him, emanating from his belief in the goodness and effective presence of his Creator. He wrote, "We admire the mechanism of a watch, and the fabric of a piece of brocade, as being the production of art; these merit our admiration, and must excite our esteem for the ingenious artist or modifier; but nature is the work of God omnipotent; and an elephant, nay even this world, is comparatively but a very minute part of his works."

There is a special, very different quality about patriot soldiers, and John McIntosh exemplified it. In blending a courageous, detached heroism and a political and spiritual dedication to country in time of peril, he resembled Andrew Jackson, Douglas MacArthur, and Winston Churchill. Like many of those of a similar point of view, McIntosh might well have said, "When my country needs me, my country right or wrong, we can always make it right later on." Any combat veteran admires such spirit. John McIntosh was squarely in the tradition of the warrior-patriot.

"Liberty is but an empty name—a mere burlesque—if we fear to speak the truth," said Zephaniah Kingsley, slave owner and erstwhile slave trader, when he spoke on slavery as a member of the Florida legislature in 1823. It is the only significant speech that has been preserved from the Florida legislature's second session. It was candid and sufficiently controversial to assure that he would never again be appointed to the legislature.

Although Kingsley's first year of service in the legislature was also his last, it was followed by a busy life of substantial private and public concerns through which he expanded his humanitarian ideals. These ideals led him to establish and fund in Haiti a haven for freed slaves and colored persons, where laws would treat all fairly and equally. Although the candor of his speech in 1823 irritated both friends and foes of slavery, what he said made it easier for the friends of liberty to move forward to end the institution of slavery. Kingsley was no saint, but he was a man of courage, and he grew in spirit and humanitarian concern.

Alfred duPont, his wife, Jessie, and brother-in-law, Ed Ball, collectively had a salutary effect on banking and other business interests in Florida. Their charitable contributions in life and testamentary provisions were diverse and outstanding. It can be accurately said of them that they dearly heeded the ancestral duPont admonition that "no privilege exists which is not inseparably bound to a duty." Of the three, Jessie was the most loved because she found it possible to touch the lives of thousands of people in a personal and uplifting manner, whether by way of charitable donations she handled herself or through unassuming and genuine friendship.

Eartha White devoted her life to helping others. She worked with quiet persuasion to enlist thousands of people in her causes for the benefit of the many needy persons she saw about her. She possessed a great capacity for bringing out in others their best qualities.

On occasion Eartha White lent her efforts to confrontational events. She helped A. Philip Randolph plan a march on Washington, for example. The march was made unnecessary when Franklin Roosevelt issued order 8802 to ban discrimination in defense and government employment, the objective she and Randolph were seeking. Her concerns were usually of a universal nature, without racial overtones: unwed mothers, tuberculosis patients, the homeless, the hungry, and others in need. She was motivated greatly by Christian concepts and the moral judgments of Clara White, her adoptive mother. They were a team, even long after Clara's death.

It is hoped that the life stories, which are told with historical accuracy in this book, may by example be helpful to the reader. Certainly each of these lives has important and spirit-lifting values. Sharing these values was the purpose of this work.

References

Abbot, W. W. 1959. *The Royal Governors of Georgia, 1754–1775*. Chapel Hill: University of North Carolina Press.

Acts of the Legislative Council of the Territory of Florida. 1829. Pensacola: John Fitzgerald.

American State Papers. 1832–61. Vol. 8: Public Lands. Washington: Gales & Stratton.

Ball, Edward. File. Charles E. Bennett Papers. University of Florida, Gainesville.

Bartram, J. 1942. Diary of a Journey through the Carolinas, Georgia, and Florida from July 1, 1765, to April 10, 1766. In *Transactions of the American Philosophical Society*, n.s. 33 (December). Philadelphia: American Philosophical Society.

Bartram, W. 1794. *Travels through North and South Carolina, Georgia, and East and West Florida* 2d ed. London: J. Johnson.

———. [1791]. 1940. *Travels through North & South Carolina, Georgia, and East & West Florida*. New York: Facsimile Library.

———. 1943. Travels in Georgia and Florida, 1773–74: A Report to Dr. John Fothergill. In *Transactions of the American Philosophical Society*, n.s. 33 (November). Philadelphia: American Philosophical Society.

——— *See also* Harper (1958).

Benjamin, S. G. W. 1878. The Sea Islands. *Harpers* (November):839–61.

Bennett, Charles E. 1964. *Laudonnière and Fort Caroline.* Gainesville: University of Florida Press.

———. 1970. *Southernmost Battlefields of the Revolution.* Bailey's Crossroads, VA: Blair, Inc.

———. 1982. *Florida's "French" Revolution, 1793–1795.* Gainesville: University Presses of Florida.

———. 1987. Most Admire Courage Displayed in Actions by Andrew Jackson. *Florida Times-Union,* 26 April.

———. Collection. Library of Congress.

———. Papers. University of Florida Library, Gainesville.

———, ed. 1968. *Settlement of Florida.* Gainesville: University of Florida Press.

———, trans. 1975. *Three Voyages,* by René Laudonnière. Gainesville: University Presses of Florida.

Bevan, J. V. n.d. Bosomworth Controversy Letters, 1743–1759. Peter Force Papers, Series 7E. Manuscript Division, Library of Congress.

Boatner, M. M., III. 1966. *Encyclopedia of the American Revolution.* New York: David McKay.

Bolton, H. E., ed. 1925. *Arredondo's Historical Proof of Spain's Title to Georgia.* Berkeley: University of California Press.

Cabell, B., and A. J. Hanna. 1943. *The St. Johns.* New York: Farrar & Rinehart.

Carr, W. H. A. 1964. *The Du Ponts of Delaware.* New York: Dodd, Mead.

Carrington, H. B. 1881. *Battles of the American Revolution.* New York: Promontory.

Carter, C. E., ed. 1959. *The Territorial Papers of the United States.* Vols. 22–24. Washington: U.S. Government Printing Office.

Cate, M. 1930. *Our Todays and Yesterdays.* Brunswick, GA: Glover Bros.

Cheek, M. T. F., and R. B. Draughon, eds. 1985. *Jessie Ball du Pont.* Stratford, VA: Robert E. Lee Memorial Association.

Child, L. M. 1970. *Letters from New York.* 3d ed. Freeport, NY: Books for Libraries.

Coker, William S. 1976. *Historical Sketches of Panton, Leslie and Company.* Pensacola: University of West Florida.

Colonial Records of the State of Georgia. 1907. Vol. 8. Atlanta: Franklin-Turner Co.

Colonial Records of the State of Georgia. 1975. Vol. 28, pt. 1. Ed. K. Coleman and M. Ready. Athens: University of Georgia Press.

Connor, J. T., ed. 1927. *The Whole & True Discouerye of Terra Flor-*

ida, by Jean Ribaut. Deland: Florida State Historical Society.

Corry, John Pitts. 1941. Some New Light on the Bosomworth Claims. *Georgia Historical Quarterly* 25 (September):195–224.

Corse, C. D. 1931. *The Key to the Golden Islands.* Chapel Hill: University of North Carolina Press.

Coulter, E. M. 1947. *Georgia, a Short History.* Chapel Hill: University of North Carolina Press.

———. 1927. Mary Musgrove, Queen of the Creeks: A Chapter of Early Georgia Troubles. *Georgia Historical Quarterly* 11 (March):1–30.

Covington, J. W., ed. 1963. *Pirates, Indians and Spaniards.* St. Petersburg, FL: Great Outdoors Publishing.

Creek Indians. File. Georgia Department of Archives and History, Atlanta.

Cumming, W. P. 1958. *The Southeast in Early Maps.* Princeton, NJ: Princeton University Press.

———. 1963. The Parreus Map (1562) of French Florida. In *Imago mundi,* 17:27–41. Amsterdam: N. Israel.

Darlington, W., ed. [1849]. 1967. *Memorials of John Bartram and Humphry Marshall.* Facsimile reprint. New York: Hafner Publishing.

Davis, T. F. 1925. *History of Jacksonville.* Jacksonville: Florida Historical Society.

———. 1928. *McGregor's Invasion of Florida, 1817.* St. Augustine: Florida Historical Society.

De Vorsey, L., Jr., ed. 1971. *De Brahm's Report of the General Survey in the Southern District of North America.* Columbia: University of South Carolina Press.

duPont, Jessie Ball. File. Charles E. Bennett Papers. University of Florida, Gainesville.

———. File. Edward Ball Building, Jacksonville.

duPont Biographical File. Charles E. Bennett Papers. University of Florida, Gainesville.

Earnest, E. 1940. *John and William Bartram, Botanists and Explorers.* Philadelphia: University of Pennsylvania Press.

Fagin, N. B. 1933. *William Bartram.* Baltimore: Johns Hopkins University Press.

Florida East Coast Railroad. Files. Charles E. Bennett Papers. University of Florida, Gainesville.

Florida Suntime, 29 August 1953.

Folmer, H. 1953. *Franco-Spanish Rivalry in North America, 1524–1763.* Glendale, CA: Arthur H. Clark.

Fretwell, J. K. 1984. Kingsley Beatty Gibbs and His Journal of 1840–1843. In *El Escribano*, 21: 53–87. St. Augustine: St. Augustine Historical Society.

Gaffarel, P. 1875. *Histoire de la Floride française*. Paris: Librairie de Firmin-Didot et cie.

———. 1878. *Histoire du Brésil français*. Paris: Maisonneuve et cie.

Gaines, F. P. 1959. *Edward Ball and the Alfred I. du Pont Tradition*. New York: Newcomen Society.

Gamble, T. [1794]. 1923. *Savannah Duels and Duelists, 1733–1877*. Savannah: Reprint Co.

Gannon, M. V. 1965. *The Cross in the Sand*. Gainesville: University of Florida Press.

Geiger, M. 1937. *The Franciscan Conquest of Florida (1573–1618)*. Washington, DC: Catholic University Press.

Georgia Department of Archives and History. Creek Indians File. Atlanta.

Gill, J. E., and B. R. Reed, eds. 1975. *Born of the Sun*. Hollywood, FL: Bicentennial Commemorative Journal.

Gold, P. D. 1929. *History of Duval County*. St. Augustine, FL: Record.

Gold, R. L. 1969. *Borderland Empires in Transition*. Carbondale: Southern Illinois University Press.

Graff, M. B. 1963. *Mandarin on the St. Johns*. Gainesville: University of Florida Press.

Grant, W. L., ed. 1907. *The History of New France*. Toronto: Champlain Society.

Griffith, L. O. 1975. *Ed Ball: Confusion to the Enemy*. Tampa: Trend House.

Haag, E., and E. Haag. 1877. *La France protestante*. Vol. 1. Paris: Librairie Sandoz et Fischbacher.

Hamer, M. B. 1929. Edmund Gray and His Settlement at New Hanover. *Georgia Historical Quarterly* 13 (March):1–55.

Harper, F. 1953. William Bartram and the American Revolution. In *Proceedings of the American Philosophical Society* 97:571–77.

———, ed. 1958. *The Travels of William Bartram, Naturalist's Edition*. New Haven: Yale University Press.

Hawes, L. M., ed. 1951. Proceedings of the President and Assistants in Council of Georgia, 1749–1751. *Georgia Historical Quarterly* 25:323–35.

Histoire mémorable de la Reprinse de L'Isle de la Floride. 1568. France.

Hitz, A. M. 1957. The Wrightsborough Quaker Town and Township in Georgia. *Bulletin of Friends Historical Association* 46:10–21.

Huxford, F. 1967. *Pioneers of Wiregrass Georgia*. Vol. 5. Waycross, GA: Herrin's Print Shop.

James, M. 1941. *Alfred I. du Pont*. Indianapolis: Bobbs-Merrill.

Johannes, J. H., Sr. 1976. *Yesterday's Reflections*. Callahan, FL: Sun Printing.

Kingsley, Z. 1834. *A Treatise on the Patriarchal System of Society, as It Exists in Some Governments and Colonies in America, and in the United States, under the Name of Slavery, with Its Necessity and Advantages*. 4th ed.

Knight, L. L. 1913. *Georgia's Landmarks, Memorials and Legends*. Atlanta: Byrd Printing.

Knox, H. 1948. Jessie Ball du Pont, Banker, Financier and Doctor of Humanities. *The Woman Banker* 24, 6 (August–September).

Lanning, J. T. 1935. *The Spanish Missions of Georgia*. Chapel Hill: University of North Carolina Press.

Legear, C. E. 1949. The Sixteenth-Century Maps Presented by Mr. Lessing J. Rosenwald. *Library of Congress Quarterly Journal of Current Acquisitions* (May):18–23.

L'Engle, G. N. 1949, 1951. *A Collection of Letters, Information and Data on Our Family*. Vols. 1 and 2. Jacksonville: privately printed.

L'Engle, S. 1888. *Notes of My Family and Recollections of My Early Life*. New York: Knickerbocker.

Lorant, S. 1946. *The New World*. New York: Duell, Sloan & Pearce.

Louisiana Historical Association. Collection. File 55N, box 2, folder 21. Tulane University, New Orleans.

Lowery, W. 1959. *The Spanish Settlements within the Present Limits of the United States: Florida, 1562-1574*. Vols. 1 and 2. New York: Russell & Russell.

McCall, H. [1811]. 1909. *The History of Georgia*. Atlanta: Cherokee Publishing.

McDowell, W. L., Jr., ed. 1958–70. *Documents Relating to Indian Affairs*. Vols. 1 and 2. Columbia, SC: Archives.

McIlvaine, P. 1971. *The Dead Town of Sunbury*. Asheville, NC: Groves Printing.

McInnis, M., ed. 1979. *Bartram Heritage*. Montgomery, AL: Bartram Trail Conference.

Mason, R., and V. Harrison. 1976. *Confusion to the Enemy: A Biography of Edward Ball*. New York: Dodd, Mead.

May, P. S. 1945. Zephaniah Kingsley, Nonconformist (1765–1843). *Florida Historical Quarterly* 22:145–59.

"Memorandum of 1797." Cochrane Papers. National Library of Scotland, Edinburgh.

Message from the President of the United States. 1817. Washington: E.D. Krafft.

Milanich, J. T., and W. C. Sturtevant. 1972. *Francisco Pareja's 1613 Confessionario*. Tallahassee: Florida Department of State.

Miller, D. H. 1918. *Secret Statutes of the United States*. Washington: Government Printing Office.

Miller, J. B. 1978. The Rebellion in East Florida in 1795. *Florida Historical Quarterly* 57 (October):173–86.

———. 1979. Juan Nepomuceno de Quesada. Ph.D. diss., Florida State University, Tallahassee.

Mosley, L. 1980. *Blood Relations*. New York: Atheneum.

Murdoch, R. K. 1951. *The Georgia-Florida Frontier, 1793–1796: Spanish Reaction to French Intrigue and American Designs*. Berkeley: University of California Press.

Oré, Luis Gerónimo de. 1936. *The Martyrs of Florida (1513–1616)*. Translated by Maynard Geiger. Franciscan Studies 18. New York: J.F. Wagner.

Owsley, Frank L., Jr. 1981. *Struggle for the Gulf Borderlands: The Creek War and the Battle of New Orleans, 1812–1815*. Gainesville: University Presses of Florida.

Papeles de Cuba, Legajo 166, pormenor 16. Archivo General de Indias, Seville.

Patrick, Rembert W. 1954. *Florida Fiasco*. Athens: University of Georgia Press.

Reese, C. L. 1977. *The Horse on Rodney Square*. Wilmington, DE: *Wilmington News-Journal*.

Ribault, Jean. *See* Connor.

Roncière, C. de la. 1923. *Histoire de la Marine française*. Vols. 3 and 4. Paris: F. Plon Nourrit, et cie.

———. 1928. *La Floride française*. Paris: Editions Nationales.

The Rural Code of Haiti. 1838. 2d ed. New York: G. Vale, Jr.

Santo Domingo. Archivo General de Indias, 87:3. Microfilm, P.K. Yonge Library, Gainesville, FL.

Schafer, D. L. 1980. Eartha Mary Magdalene White. In *Notable American Women*, 726–28. Cambridge: Harvard University Press.

———. 1976. Eartha White: The Early Years of a Jacksonville Humanitarian. University of North Florida, Jacksonville. Typescript.

Smith, T. E. V. 1891. Villegaignon. *Report and Papers of the Third Annual Meeting of the American Society of Church History*. Vol. 3. New York: G. P. Putnam's Sons.

Snodgrass, D. 1969a. The Birth of a City. In *Papers of the Jacksonville Historical Society*, vol. 5.

———. 1969b. Fort George Island. In *Papers of the Jacksonville Historical Society*, vol. 5.

———. 1969c. Spain and the McIntoshes of Georgia. In *Papers of the Jacksonville Historical Society*, vol. 5.

Sparks, J. 1845. John Ribault. *Library of American Biography*. Vol. 17. Boston: Little Brown.

State of Florida. Archives. Tallahassee: Office of the Secretary of State.

Stephens, J. B. 1978. Zephaniah Kingsley and the Recaptured Africans. In *El Escribano*. St. Augustine: St. Augustine Historical Society.

Superior Court of East Florida. *United States* v. *Zephaniah Kingsley*. 37 U.S. Reports 476.

Territorial Papers of Florida. Vol. 3. Microfilm (M116, roll 3). Manuscripts Division, Library of Congress.

Thevêt, A. [1575]. 1953. *Les Français en Amérique*. [Paris: Huillier.] Reprint. Paris: University Presses of Paris.

U.S. Congress. Senate. *U.S.* v. *Ferreira*. 36th Cong., 1st sess. S. Misc. Doc. 55.

Ward, J. R. (with Dena Snodgrass). 1982. *Old Hickory's Town*. Jacksonville: Florida Publishing.

Watt, M.G. 1968. *Tenax Propositii. The Gibbs Family of Long Ago and Near at Hand, 1337–1967*. St. Augustine, FL: privately printed.

White, Eartha. Collection. University of North Florida, Jacksonville.

White, G. 1849. *Statistics of the State of Georgia*. Savannah: W. Thorne Williams.

———. 1855. *Historical Collections of Georgia*. New York: Pudney & Russell.

Who Was Who in America. 1973. Chicago: A. N. Marquis.

Williams, J. L. [1837]. 1962. *The Territory of Florida*. Facsimile reproduction. Gainesville: University of Florida Press.

Wright, J. L., Jr. 1966. British Designs on the Old Southwest: Foreign Intrigue on the Florida Frontier. *Florida Historical Quarterly* 44 (April):265–84.

———. 1981. *The Only Land They Knew*. New York: Free Press.

Index

Numbers in italics refer to illustrations.

161